FREE AUDIO EXAMPLES
Available for Streaming or Download –
No Sign-up Required!

HOW TO PLAY UKULELE IN 14 DAYS!
Daily Ukulele Lessons for Beginners
By Michael Mueller
Edited by Troy Nelson

HOW TO GET THE AUDIO	3		
INTRODUCTION	4		
HOW TO USE THIS BOOK	5		
THE UKULELE, TUNING, TAB & CHORD DIAGRAMS	6		
UKULELE CHORDS	9		
DAY 1	10	DAY 8	33
DAY 2	13	DAY 9	36
DAY 3	16	DAY 10	39
DAY 4	19	DAY 11	43
DAY 5	22	DAY 12	47
DAY 6	25	DAY 13	50
DAY 7: WEEK 1 REVIEW PUTTING IT ALL TOGETHER	29	DAY 14: WEEK 2 REVIEW: PUTTING IT ALL TOGETHER	54

ISBN 9781672893381   Copyright © 2019 Michael Mueller and Troy Nelson Music
International Copyright Secured. All Rights Reserved

No part of this publication may be reproduced without the written consent of the author, Michael Mueller, and publisher, Troy Nelson Music. Unauthorized copying, arranging, adapting, recording, Internet posting, public performance or other distribution of the printed or recorded music in this publication is an infringement of copyright. Infringers are liable under the law.

HOW TO GET THE AUDIO

The audio files for this book are available for free as downloads or streaming on *troynelsonmusic.com*.

We are available to help you with your audio downloads and any other questions you may have. Simply email *help@troynelsonmusic.com*.

See below for the recommended ways to listen to the audio:

Download Audio Files (Zipped)	Stream Audio Files
• Download Audio Files (Zipped)	• Recommended for CELL PHONES & TABLETS
• Recommended for COMPUTERS on WiFi	• Bookmark this page
• A ZIP file will automatically download to the default "downloads" folder on your computer	• Simply tap the PLAY button on the track you want to listen to
• Recommended to download to a desktop/laptop computer *first* before transferring to a tablet or cell phone	• Files also available for streaming or download at *soundcloud.com/troynelsonbooks*
• Phones & tablets may need an "unzipping" app such as iZip, Unrar or Winzip	
• Download on WiFi for faster download speeds	

**To download the companion audio files for this book,
visit: troynelsonmusic.com/audio-downloads/**

INTRODUCTION

Congratulations on your decision to learn how to play the ukulele! Due to its relative ease to play, portability, and sheer fun factor, the ukulele has become one of the most popular instruments of the past decade, heard everywhere from tween bedrooms and school talent shows to street-corner buskers and the biggest concert stages.

The ukulele—properly pronounced in Hawaiian as "oo-koo-lay-lay"—had its humble beginnings on the streets of late 19th-century Hawaii. It later found a larger audience on the vaudeville stages of the early 20th century. Then, after flying under the radar for a couple of decades, Tiny Tim's 1968 falsetto-fueled "Tiptoe Through the Tulips" reminded the world just how much fun the little instrument could be. But, it was the prodigious mastery of Jake Shimabukuro and his 2006 cover of "While My Guitar Gently Weeps" that turned music lovers' attention back to the instrument. And, more recently, it was then-12-year-old Grace VanderWaal and her stunning 2016 performance of "I Don't Know My Name" on the NBC hit television show "America's Got Talent" that inspired millions of young people to pick up the ukulele and make music.

Over the past 10 years, the ukulele has gone from being largely viewed as a novelty for kids to one of the most popular instruments in the world. According to figures from the National Association of Music Merchants, ukulele sales have risen nearly 400% over the past decade, and it's still growing. In many elementary schools, the ukulele has taken the place of the somewhat antiquated recorder as the primary tool for teaching children the basics of music. A growing number of private music teachers are advising parents to have their kids start with a ukulele rather than guitar. Even seasoned guitar players are picking it up to expand their own musical horizons.

How to Play Ukulele in 14 Days is methodically designed to teach you all the essential chords, strum patterns, and basic fingerpicking skills you'll need to play your favorite songs. The book is divided into 14 lessons, one for each day of the two-week program. Each day, you'll work on six exercises that focus individually on different chord types (major, minor, or dominant), strum patterns, chord progressions, fingerstyle approaches, or special techniques like muted strums, cheat strums, plucking, roll strokes, and more. The goal is to spend 10 minutes practicing each exercise, for a total of 60 minutes (10 X 6 = 60) per day. A couple of exceptions are on Day 7 and Day 14. On Day 7, the full 60 minutes are devoted to practicing the chords and melody to the folk song "Aura Lee," while Day 14 is dedicated to learning a chord-melody arrangement of the traditional song "Amazing Grace."

Because the ukulele is primarily a rhythm instrument used to accompany a singer, heavy emphasis is placed on chords and strumming technique. Further, the book dedicates a lot of space in the second week to learning popular chord progressions so that you can begin to recognize how chords are put together in the songs you want to play.

HOW TO USE THIS BOOK

Granted, 60 minutes of practice per day can seem daunting to some, especially if you are unaccustomed to practice sessions lasting longer than 20–30 minutes. And that's OK! Just because the book is structured to teach you ukulele in 14 days doesn't mean you have to follow the program precisely. On the contrary, if you have, say, 20 minutes to devote to the book each day, then simply extend each lesson to a three-day practice session. The material is there for you to use, whether you get through the book in 14 days or 40.

While the 14-day plan is the goal, it's probably unrealistic for some. The important thing is to stick with it, because the material in this book will have you playing the ukulele with confidence and credibility. How quickly just depends on the amount of time you're able to spend on getting there.

Before you begin your daily sessions, however, I suggest spending at least 15–20 minutes listening to the accompanying audio to get a feel for the forthcoming exercises, as well as reading the text in each section for some pointers and to better understand the material you're about to learn. That way, you can spend the full 60 minutes (or however much time you have to practice that day) practicing the actual exercises.

To help you keep track of time in your practice sessions, time codes are included throughout the book. Simply set the timer on your smart phone to 60 minutes (1:00)—or however much time you can dedicate to your session—and move on to a new category every 10 minutes. Or you can set the timer to 10 minutes (0:10) and move on to the next category when the timer goes off.

Next, set your metronome (or drum loop, click track, etc.) to a tempo at which you can play the exercise all the way through without making too many mistakes (60–72 beats per minute is probably a good starting point for most exercises). Once you're able to play the exercise cleanly, increase your tempo by 6–12 BPM. Again, make sure you can play through the exercise without making too many mistakes. If the speed is too fast, back off a bit until your execution is precise. Continue to increase your tempo incrementally until it's time to move on to the next section.

There will be times when the timer goes off but you feel like you didn't adequately learn the material. When this happens, I suggest moving on to the next category nonetheless. It may seem counterintuitive, but It's better to continue to progress through the book than to prolong the practice session while trying to perfect the material. After you've completed the book, you can always go back and review the exercises. In fact, I recommend it. Making steady progress, while not always perfectly, keeps you mentally sharp and motived. Focusing too much on any one exercise is a sure way to sidetrack your sessions. Plus, you'll find that, when you go back and review the old exercises, you'll almost certainly be able to play them better after having gone through the rest of the book than you would have if you'd kept working on them in your initial practice session.

Lastly—and this is important—if you ever feel yourself getting physically fatigued or pain develops in any part of your body, immediately take a break until the discomfort subsides, whether it's for 10 minutes, an hour, or for the rest of the day. You never want to push yourself beyond your physical limits and cause permanent damage. As mentioned earlier, the material isn't going anywhere; you can always go back to it when you're feeling 100%.

THE UKULELE, TUNING, TAB & CHORD DIAGRAMS

The most popular ukulele type is the *concert* size, followed by the *tenor* (pictured below), which is slightly larger than a concert (and the type that is used to record the audio examples that accompany this book), and then the *soprano*, which is slightly smaller than the concert size. The following diagram identifies all the main parts of the ukulele.

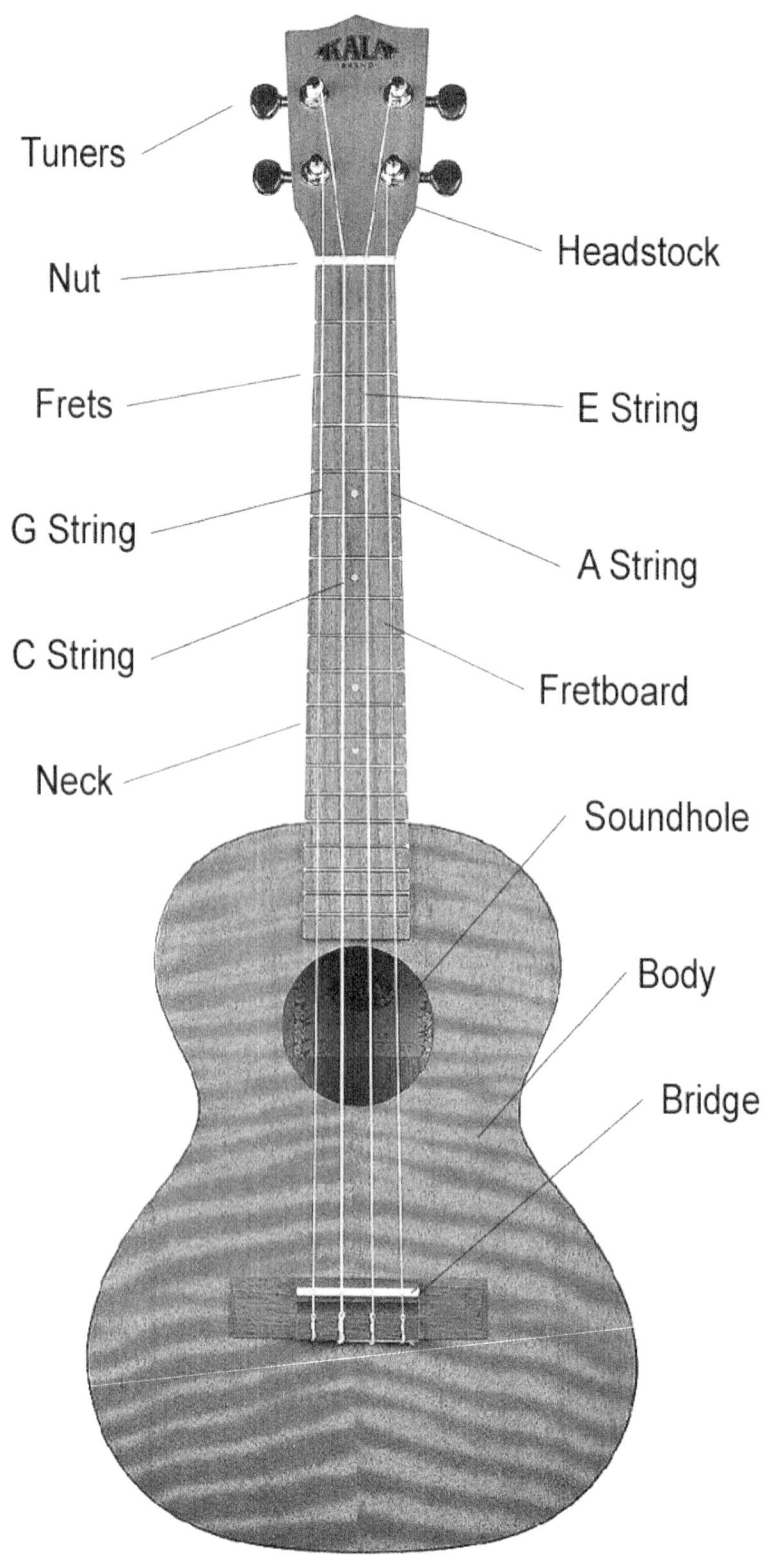

Despite their size differences, the concert, tenor, and soprano ukuleles are all tuned to the same pitches. The standard tuning for the concert, tenor, and soprano ukuleles is G–C–E–A, moving from the string closest to the ceiling to the string closest to the floor. An alternative naming pattern that you'll see throughout this book is to use string numbers:

G = 4th String
C = 3rd String
E = 2nd String
A = 1st String

Note, however, that ukulele tuning does *not* follow the "lowest pitch to highest pitch" pattern that you see on a guitar, bass, or violin. Instead, the C string is the lowest pitch, followed by the E, then the G, and then the A. Use the tuning notes on the audio track, which are played in the G–C–E–A order, as your guide.

TUNING NOTES: G–C–E–A

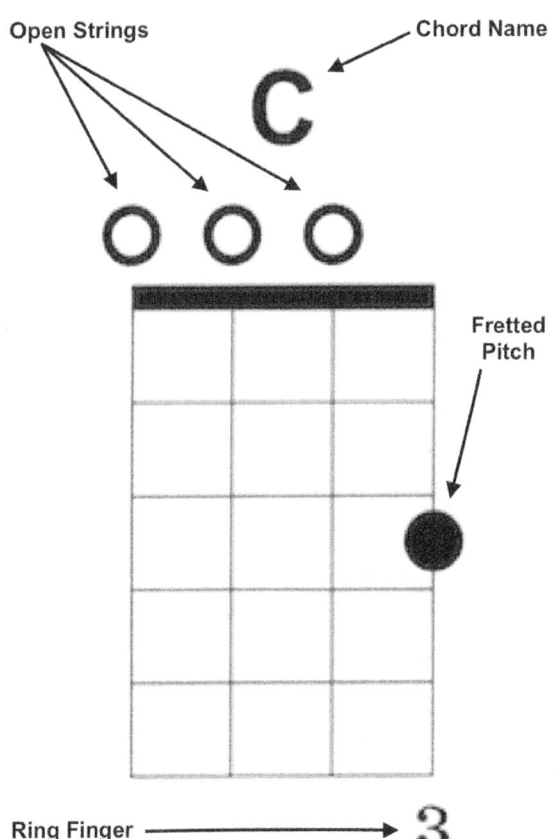

Next, you need to learn how to interpret chord diagrams, which show you on which strings and where on your ukulele's fretboard you'll find the notes of any given chord, as well as which fingers you should use to fret the notes. The four vertical lines of the diagram represent the four strings of the ukulele: G–C–E–A, from left to right. The horizontal lines represent the frets of the ukulele, with an extra-thick line at the top indicating the nut, which is the plastic piece the strings pass over before going to the tuning pegs. The dots on the diagram show you where to place your fingers to form the given chord, while any open circles above the nut indicate the string should be played open. If you see an "X" above the nut, that string should not be played.

The chord diagram displayed here shows you how to play a C major chord. The three open circles over the G, C, and E strings mean those strings should be played open, and the dot at the 3rd fret of the A string, along with the numeral "3" beneath the frame, indicates that you should use your 3rd (ring) finger to hold down the A string at the 3rd fret while playing the chord.

7

On the next page, you'll find a quick-reference guide to popular ukulele chords, which also corresponds with the ones you'll learn throughout this book.

Finally, this book uses a numeric notation system called *tablature*, or *tab*, rather than standard music notation for all of the music examples. In tab, the four horizontal lines represent the four strings of the ukulele. The top line is the A string, second line is E, third is C, and fourth, or bottom, is G. You'll also see "stems," commonly associated with standard music notation, attached to the tab to indicate the rhythm with which each note is played. Below you'll find the most common rhythms, including quarter notes, half notes, whole notes, eighth notes, and triplets, as well as rhythmic devices such as rests, ties, and more.

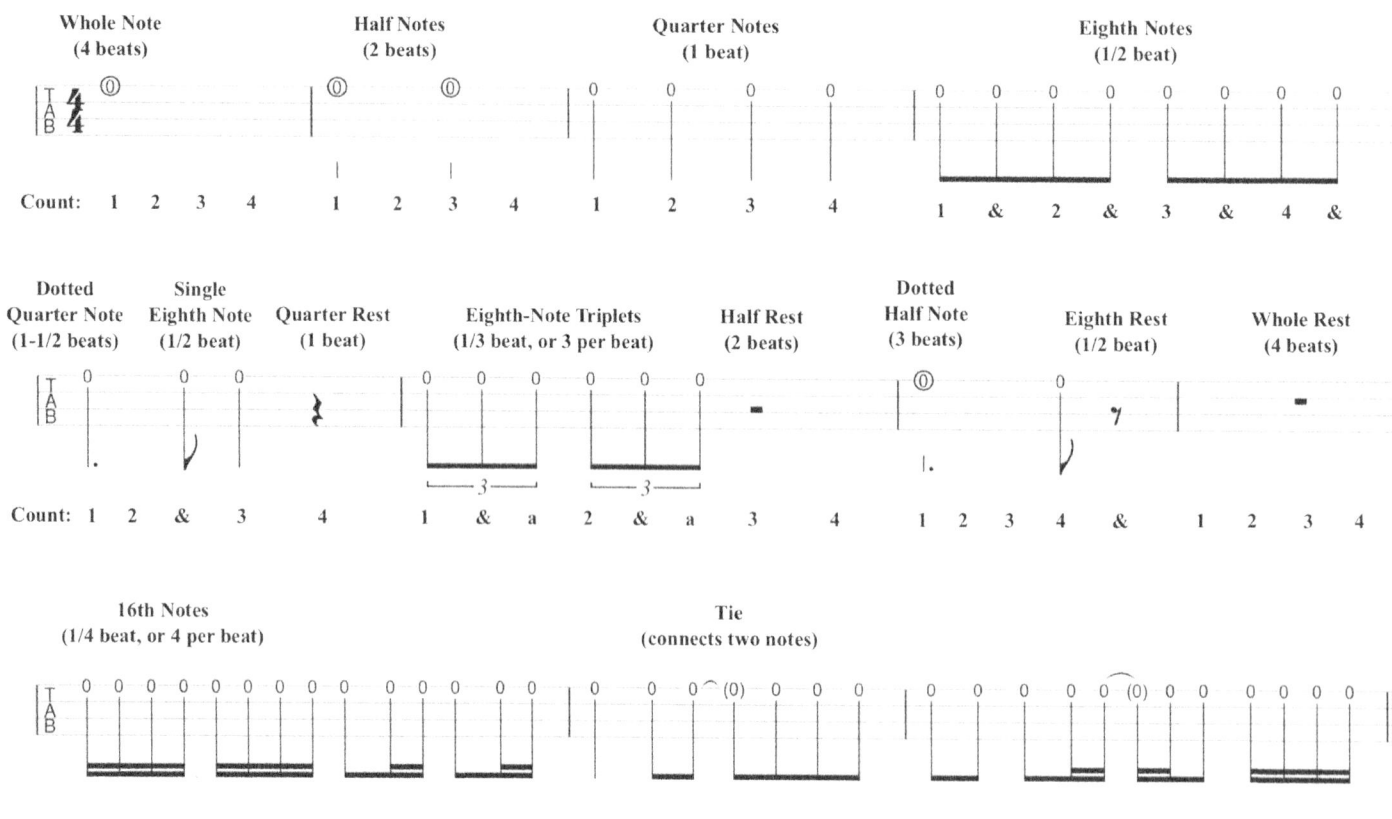

8

UKULELE CHORDS

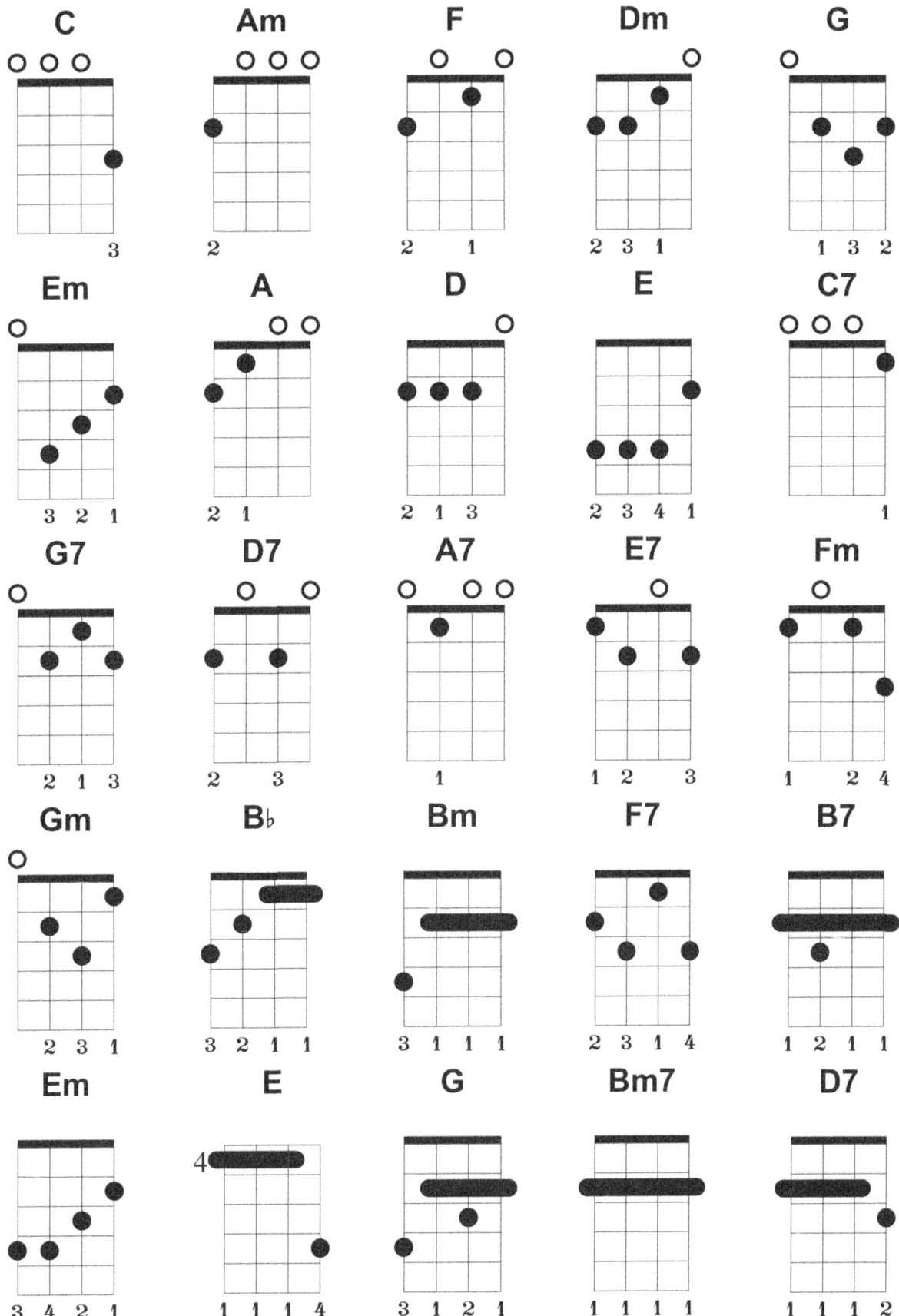

DAY 1

MAJOR CHORD (1:00–0:50)

The first—and arguably easiest—chord you'll learn to play on the ukulele is C major. Place your ring (3rd) finger on the high A string at the 3rd fret. Press down just enough to sound the note, and then strum all four strings in a downward motion, using your right hand's thumb. This example uses half notes, so count two beats per strum; that is, while counting "1–2–3–4," you'll strum on beats 1 and 3 in each measure.

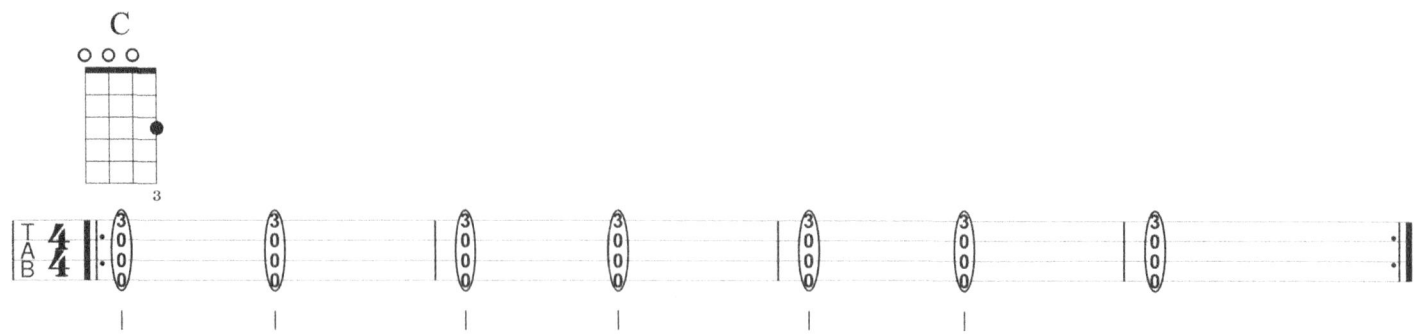

MINOR CHORD (0:50–0:40)

Like the C major chord, the A minor (Am) chord also requires just one finger. For this one, place your fret hand's middle (2nd) finger on the G string at the 2nd fret. Press down just enough so that the fretted note sounds clearly. Then strum all four strings in a downward motion, again using your right hand's thumb and in a half-note rhythm.

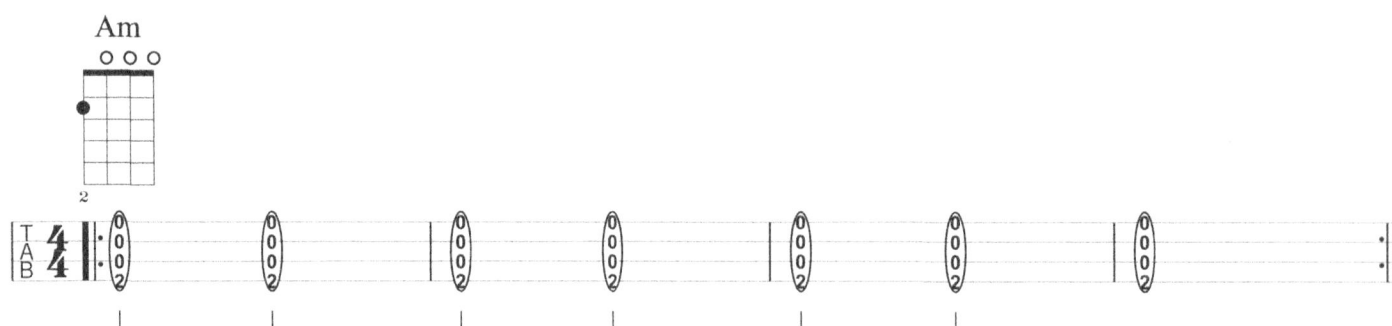

10

SEVENTH CHORD (0:40–0:30)

Seventh chords can be major, minor, or dominant, but it's the latter that you will most often hear in pop, rock, blues, and country songs. Your first dominant seventh chord is G7. Even though this one requires three fingers to form the shape, it's actually rather easy. Look at the chord diagram to see which fingers go on which strings, and once you have them firmly in place, strum all four strings in a downward motion with your thumb.

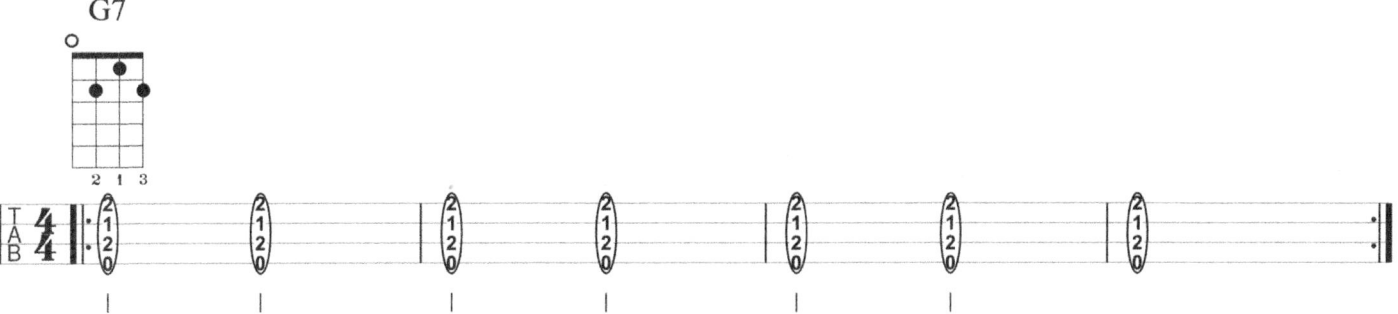

STRUM PATTERN (0:30–0:20)

Strumming is far and away the most popular technique used to play the ukulele. On its surface, strumming appears to be a strictly right-hand technique, but you have to remember that executing the strum is only half the battle when playing songs; you also need to make all the chord changes with your left hand while keeping time with the strums. With that in mind, this first strum pattern is a very simple, repeating pattern of half- and quarter-note strums on C, Am, and G7 chords. The trickiest change will be from the Am to G7, so, if you have trouble, try practicing just that change until it feels natural before including the C chord.

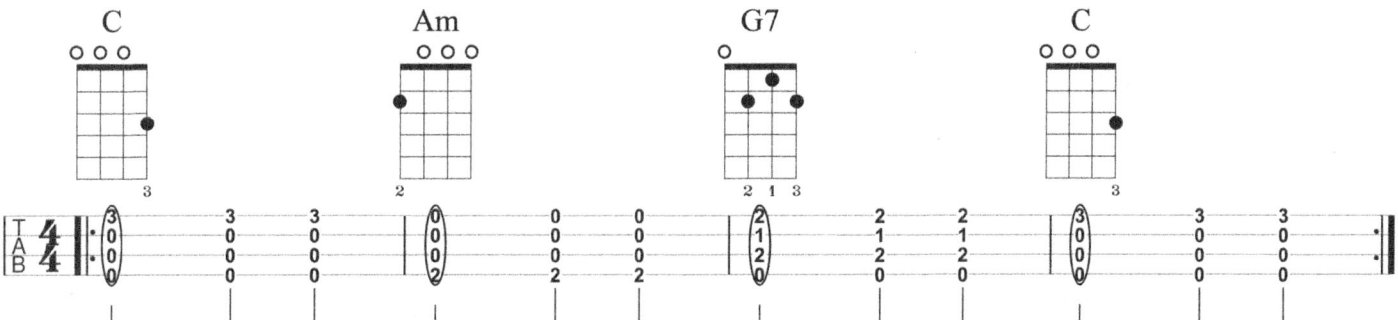

FINGERSTYLE PATTERN (0:20–0:10)

In addition to strumming chords, you will sometimes need to play them one note at a time, using your thumb, index, middle, and ring fingers. In classical guitar, each of those fingers is assigned a letter: thumb = *p*, index = *i*, middle = *m*, and ring = *a*. These four letters are then used to indicate various fingerpicking patterns. For example, the first one presented here is an ascending pattern called *"pima,"* meaning you pluck the notes of the chord from the 4th string to the 1st string, in order, with your thumb, index, middle, and ring fingers.

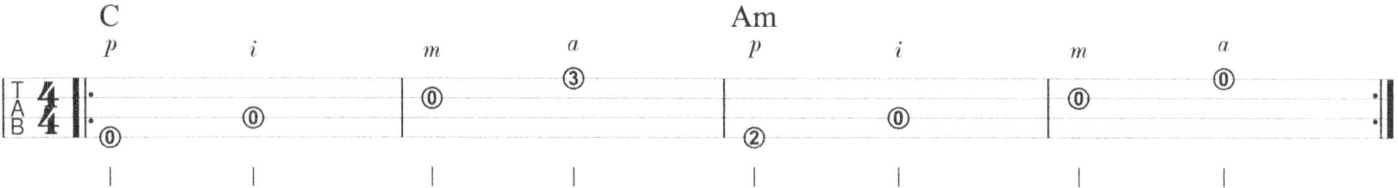

TECHNIQUE: SINGLE NOTES (0:10–0:00)

Of course, you won't just play chords on the ukulele; you'll also use single notes to play song melodies. Those melodies are derived from musical scales, typically either *major* or *minor*. Below, you'll find the C major scale, beginning on the lowest C note found on the ukulele and ending on the C note that is one *octave,* or eight notes, higher. Use your thumb to pluck each note. As for which fingers to use to fret the notes, your index finger gets all the notes on the 1st fret, your middle finger the ones on the 2nd fret, and your ring finger the ones on the 3rd fret.

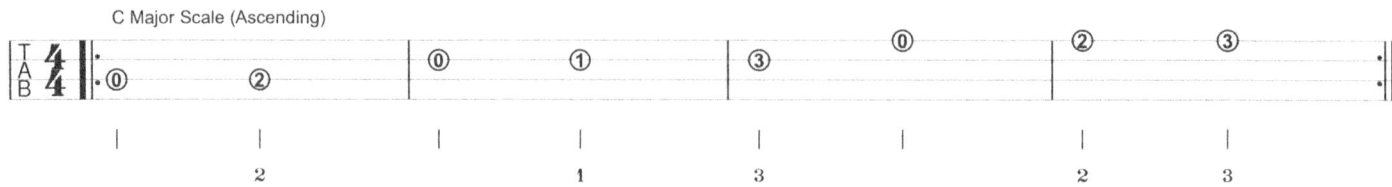

12

DAY 2

MAJOR CHORD (1:00–0:50)

Congratulations on getting through Day 1! Now let's tackle Day 2. Today's major chord is F. To play F major, place your fret hand's middle finger on the 4th string at the 2nd fret, and your index finger on the 2nd string at the 1st fret. Then use your right hand's thumb to strum all four strings in a downward motion. Be sure to keep your fret-hand fingers properly arched so that they don't accidentally mute the open 1st and 3rd strings.

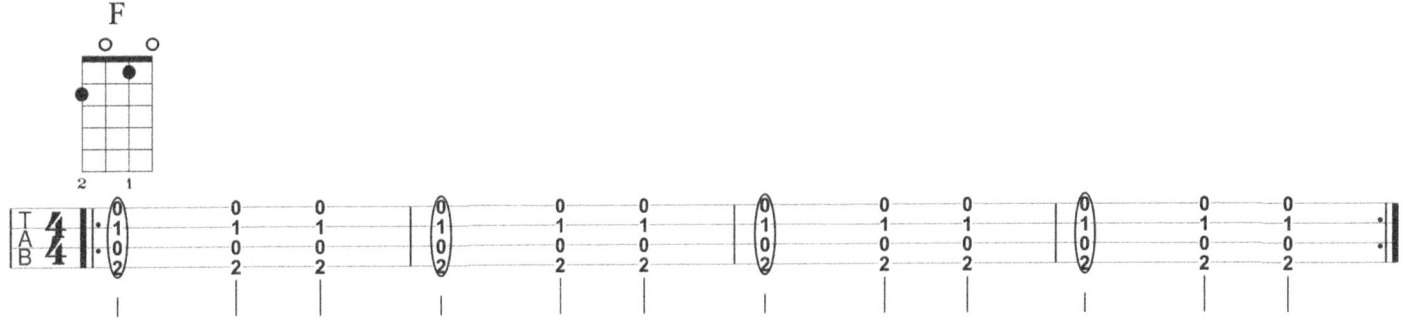

MINOR CHORD (0:50–0:40)

The Dm chord is very similar to F major; in fact, to play it, first put your fingers in position to play F major, and then add your ring finger to the 2nd fret of the 3rd string. Once you've got that down, strum all four strings in downward fashion. Did all the notes ring clearly? If not, do a chord check; that is, hold the chord shape down and play each note individually to find out which one is giving you trouble. Once you isolate that, adjust the arch of your finger or its placement along the string to allow it to ring out loud and clear. You can use the chord check on any chord that gives you trouble.

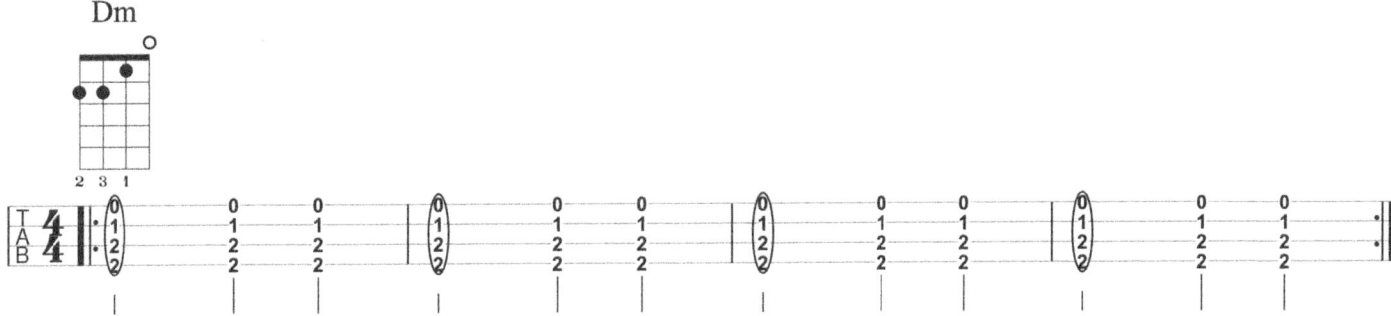

SEVENTH CHORD (0:40–0:30)

OK, it's time to learn another easy and useful one-finger chord. The C7 chord requires only your index finger, placed at the 1st fret on the 1st string. When you have that firmly in place, strum all four strings.

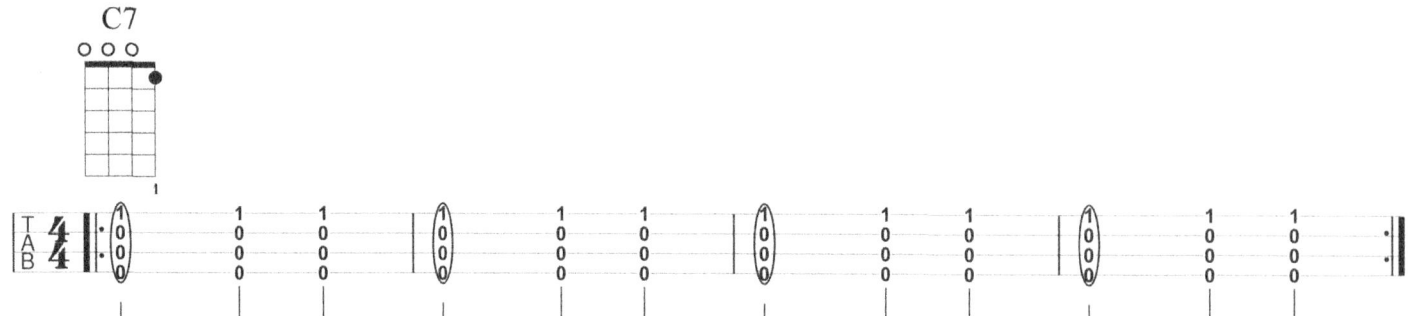

Music Theory Tip: C7 is the V ("five") chord of F major, meaning it's the chord formed from the 5th note of the F major scale, C. Though the music theory behind this isn't essential knowledge for someone on Day 2 of a lesson program, it's helpful to understand that, in many popular songs you might learn to play, the V chord is often used to lead back to the I ("one") chord—in this case, F. Likewise, the G7 you learned yesterday is the V chord of C major. Play these V–I ("five-one") sequences, like G7–C or C7–F, often so you learn to recognize them in songs you want to learn.

STRUM PATTERN (0:30–0:20)

Today's strum pattern is set in a basic quarter-note rhythm; that is, one strum per beat. This is a very simple pattern, but you have to make several chord changes along the way, which should present a small challenge. Notice how the C7 (V) chord is used in this example to perfectly lead back to the F (I) chord.

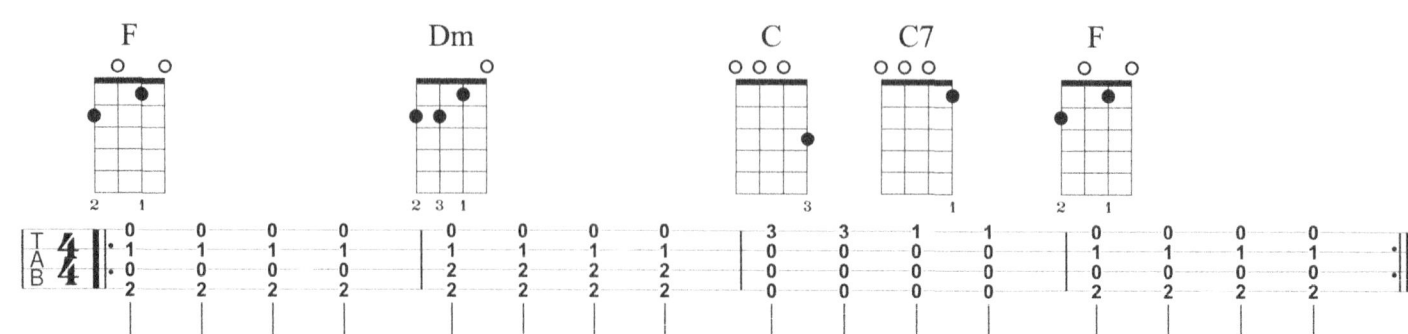

FINGERSTYLE PATTERN (0:20–0:10)

Today's fingerstyle pattern is simply the opposite of yesterday's ascending pattern, but using the F and C7 chords. This descending pattern is played *amip* (ring, middle, index, and thumb, respectively), and in a half-note rhythm just like yesterday's exercise.

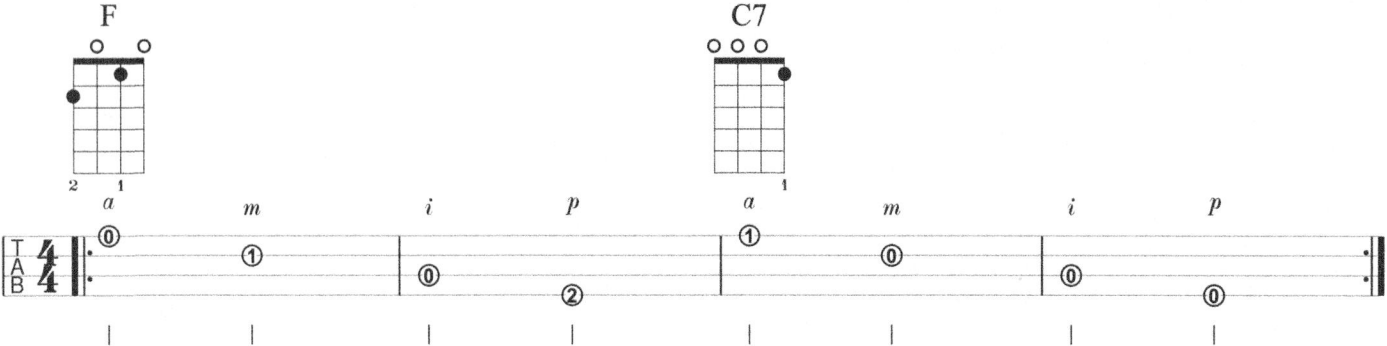

TECHNIQUE: SINGLE NOTES (0:10–0:00)

Today's single-note exercise revisits the C major scale you learned yesterday, only in *descending* order (i.e., from the highest pitch to the lowest). As before, use your thumb to pluck each note of the scale, and remember to hold each note for two whole beats.

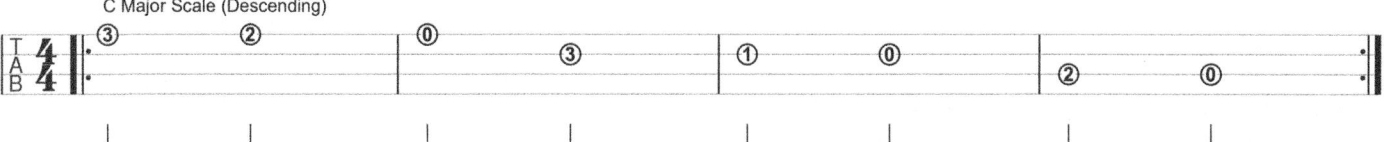

DAY 3

MAJOR CHORD (1:00–0:50)

When you learned the G7 chord, you might have noticed that your fingers formed a triangle shape. For today's G major chord, you'll be forming the mirror-image triangle. This one tends to be a little difficult for beginning ukulele players, but it's such an important and frequently used chord, it's worth taking the time to get it right. Plus, you're really going to need to have this one down when we get to some fun moves in next week's lesson plan.

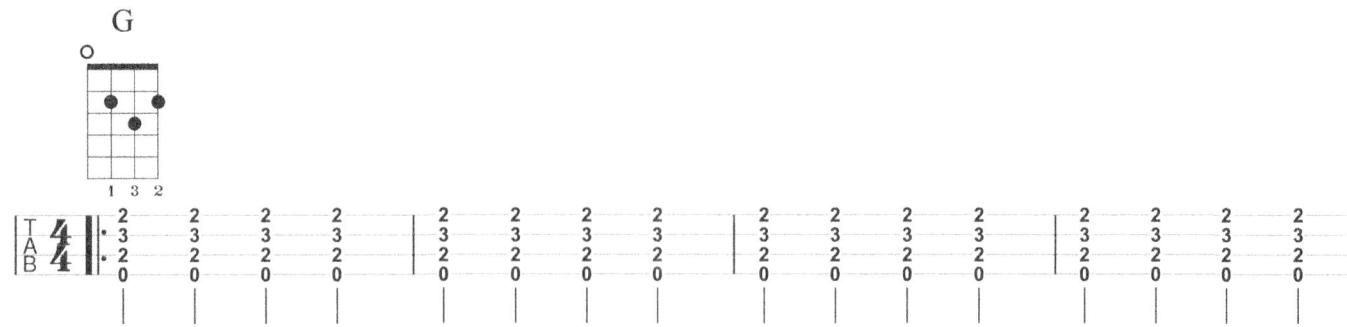

MINOR CHORD (0:50–0:40)

The Em chord features a "stair-steps" shape, as you'll see in the chord diagram. Because of the way it sits on the fretboard, this is a chord on which beginners sometimes accidentally mute strings that need to ring. If all four strings aren't ringing clearly for you, perform the chord check and adjust the arch of your fingers as needed.

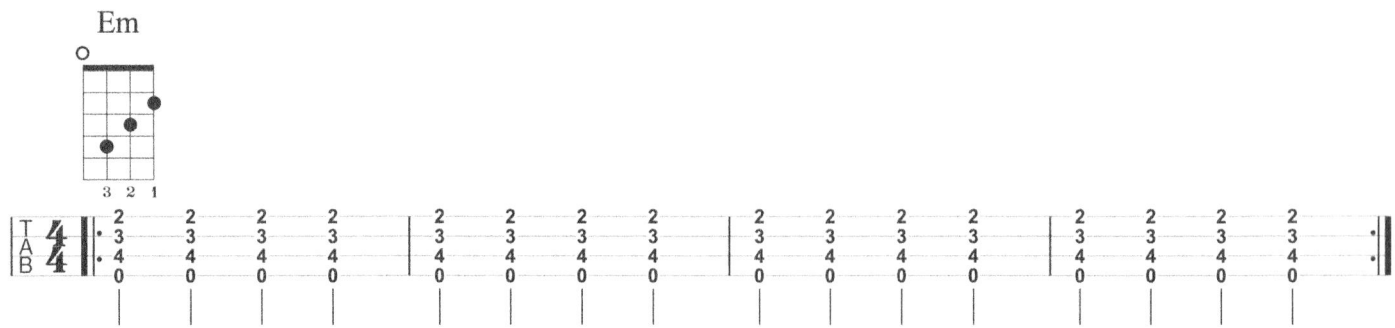

Music Theory Tip: The Em chord is the vi ("six") chord" of G major (lowercase Roman numerals represent minor chords). That means it's the chord constructed from the sixth note of the G major scale, and thus is often found in songs and chord progressions set in the key of G. Likewise, Am is the vi chord of C major (Day 1), and Dm is the vi chord of F major (Day 2).

SEVENTH CHORD (0:40–0:30)

The D7 chord is the V chord of G major, so you'll often see it in pop, country, and folk songs that are written in the key of G. There is actually another, more popular version of D7 frequently played on ukulele, but this one is easier for beginners. You'll learn the other one later in this book. Use your middle finger on the 2nd fret of string 4, and your ring finger on the 2nd fret of string 2.

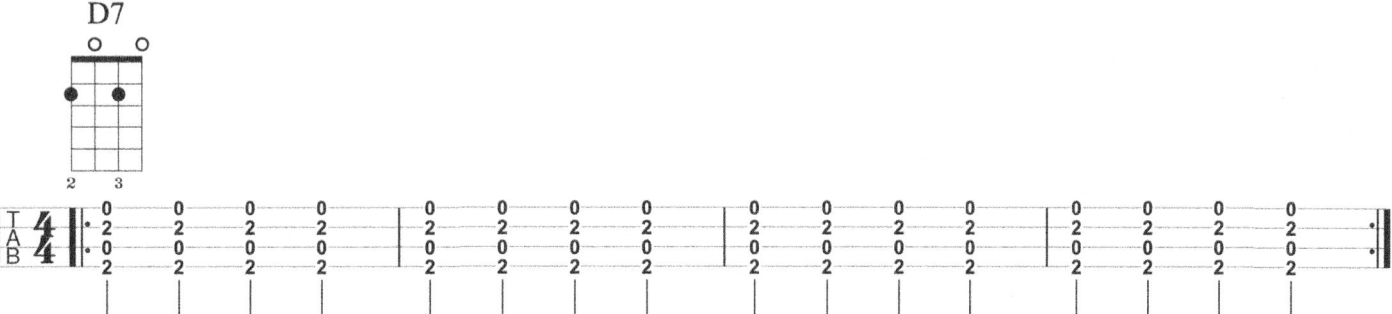

STRUM PATTERN (0:30–0:20)

Today's strum pattern introduces an eighth-note rhythm on beat 3 of each bar. So far, you've only had to strum in a downward motion, but for the eighth-note pair, you'll want to strum down on beat 3, and then strum up on the upbeat that occupies the space between beats 3 and 4. You can play the upstrum either with the side of your thumb or with the fleshy end of your index finger. Note, too, that the chord progression used in this example, G–Em–C–D7, is very commonly heard in popular music.

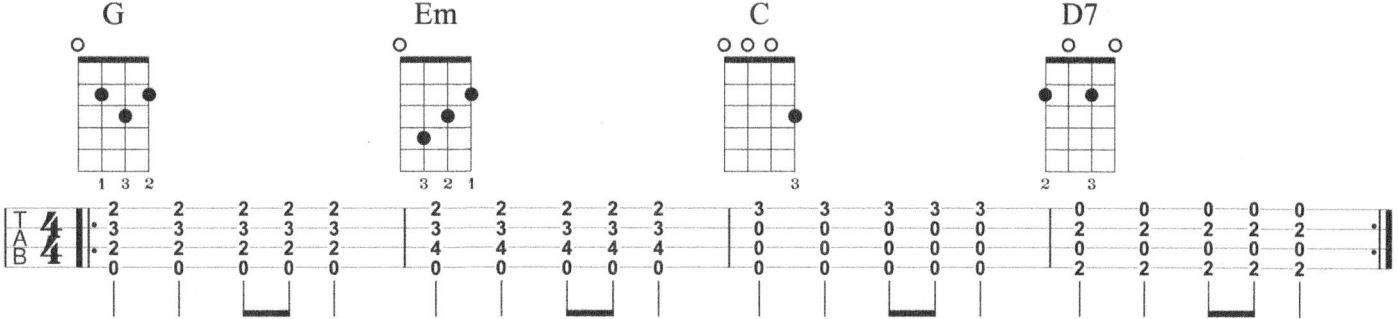

17

FINGERSTYLE PATTERN (0:20–0:10)

For today's fingerstyle pattern, let's return to the ascending *pima* pattern from Day 1, only this time it's in a quarter-note rhythm and the chords change each measure. Take this one real slow and work on maintaining that steady quarter-note rhythm—even while making the chord changes.

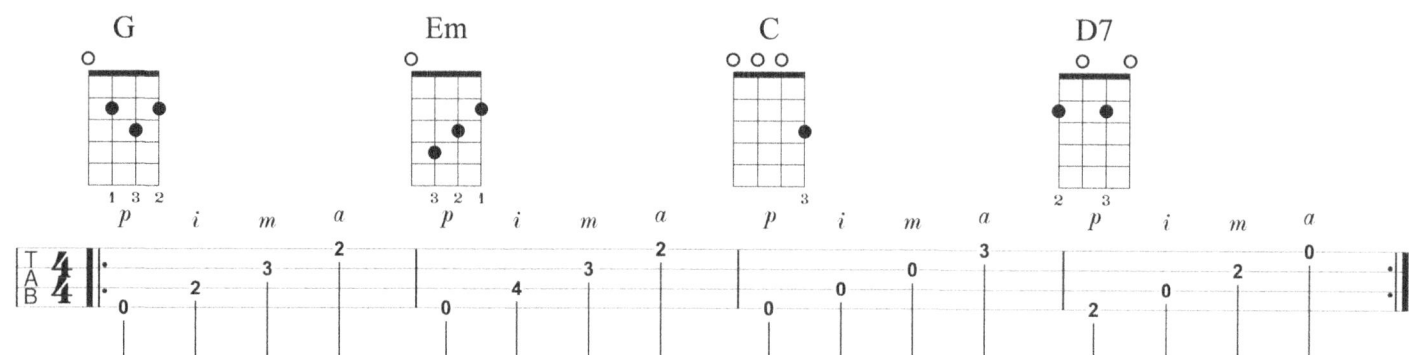

TECHNIQUE: SINGLE NOTES (0:10–0:00)

On Day 1, you played the C major scale in ascending fashion, going from low to high in pitch. Then, on Day 2, you played the same scale but in reverse. So, today, you're going to play the scale in both directions—*and* you're going to do it in a quarter-note rhythm, so it will feel twice as fast. As with the previous scales, play along with the audio first, and if you're comfortable with that tempo, you can play it faster, using a metronome or by tapping your foot.

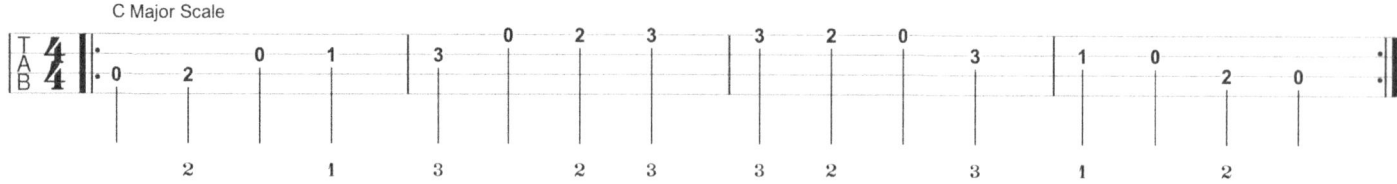

18

DAY 4

MAJOR CHORD (1:00–0:50)

Today's new major chord is A major. To play it, start by placing your fret hand's middle finger on the 4th string at the 2nd fret, as if you were going to play Am. Next, place your index finger on the 3rd string at the 1st fret, leaving strings 2–1 to ring open. Strum all four strings in a downward motion, making sure that each rings loud and clear.

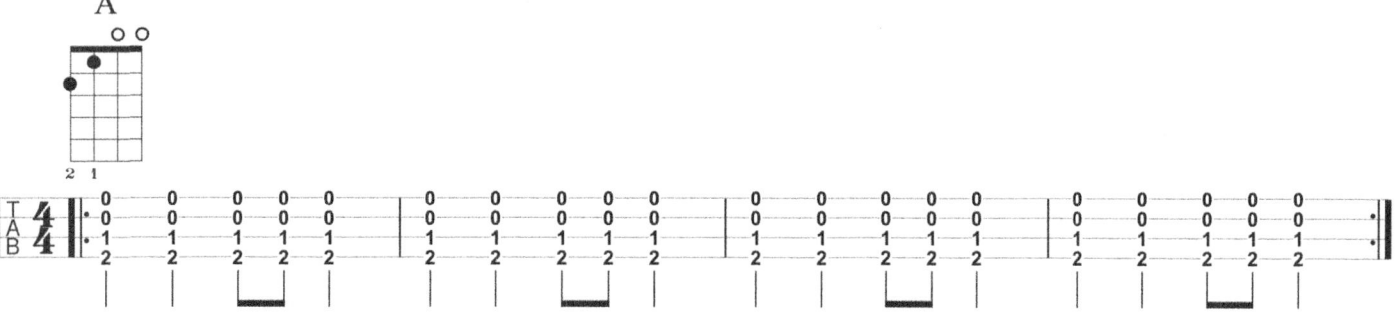

MINOR CHORD (0:50–0:40)

You've already learned how to play G7 and G major; now it's time to learn Gm. The Gm chord is different from G major by just one note; that is, the note on the 1st string is played at the 1st fret, rather than at the 2nd. But this small change necessitates a whole new fingering, as you can see in the chord diagram. Use your index finger for that 1st-fret note on the 1st string, your middle finger for the 2nd-fret note on the 3rd string, and your ring finger for the 3rd-fret note on the 2nd string.

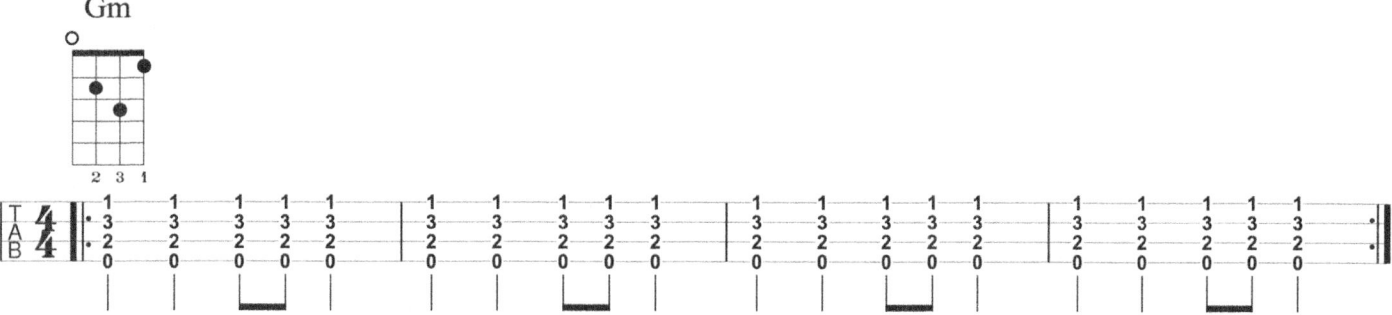

SEVENTH CHORD (0:40–0:30)

Your seventh chord for Day 4 is E7, which is the V chord in the key of A, so it goes nicely with the A major chord you just learned. To play E7, place your fret hand's index finger at the 1st fret of string 4, your middle finger at the 2nd fret of string 3, and your ring finger at the 2nd fret of string 1, leaving string 2 to ring open.

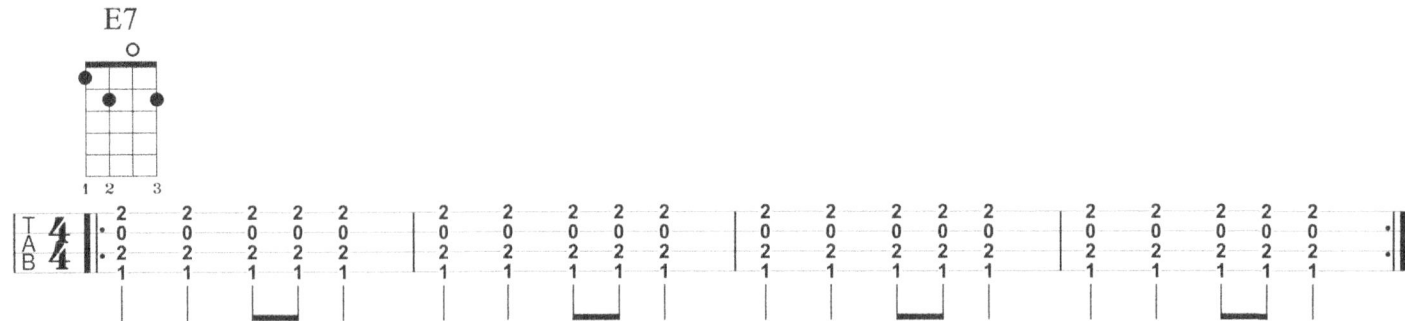

STRUM PATTERN (0:30–0:20)

Today's strum pattern is a very popular expansion on yesterday's pattern. Here, you'll play quarter-note downstrums on beats 1 and 2, and then all eighth-note strums on beats 3 and 4. The tricky part here is that, with the upstrum that now occurs during beat 4, you've got less time to make the change to the next chord, so start slowly and focus on making each chord change cleanly, without missing any strums.

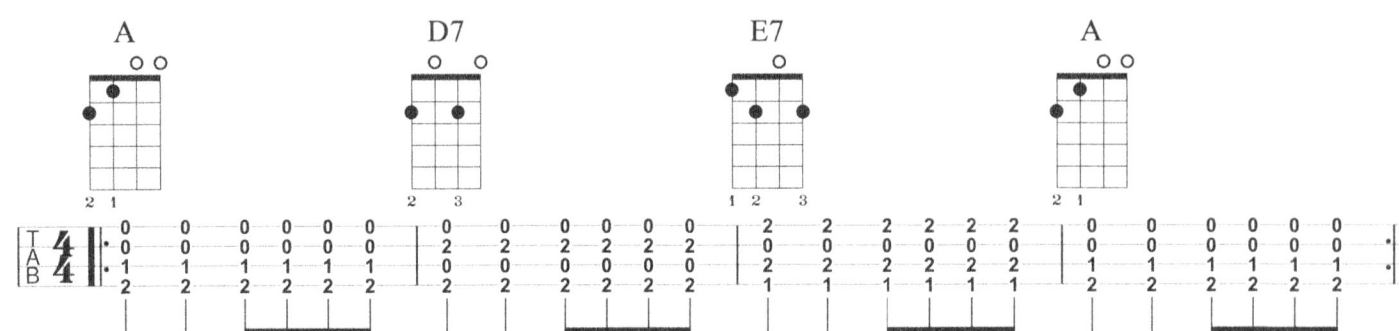

FINGERSTYLE PATTERN (0:20–0:10)

Yesterday, you learned an ascending *pima* fingerstyle pattern in a quarter-note rhythm, or one pluck per beat. Today's exercise reverses the pattern, going *amip* in descending fashion, using a Gm–C progression.

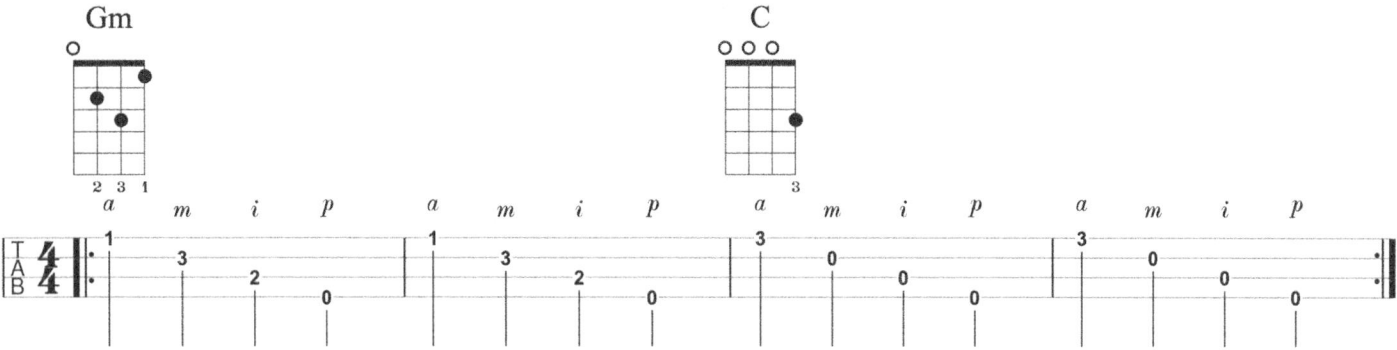

TECHNIQUE: THE SHUFFLE RHYTHM (0:10–0:00)

Now that you've learned how to strum straight eighth notes, it's time to learn the *shuffle* rhythm. Commonly heard in blues and jazz music, the shuffle is an eighth-note strum pattern but, instead of dividing the beat into two parts (counted: "one-and, two-and," etc.), you divide it into three parts and strum down on the first subdivision and up on the third subdivision ("*one*-and-*uh*, *two*-and-*uh*," etc.). Listen closely to the audio example for that slight delay on all the upbeats.

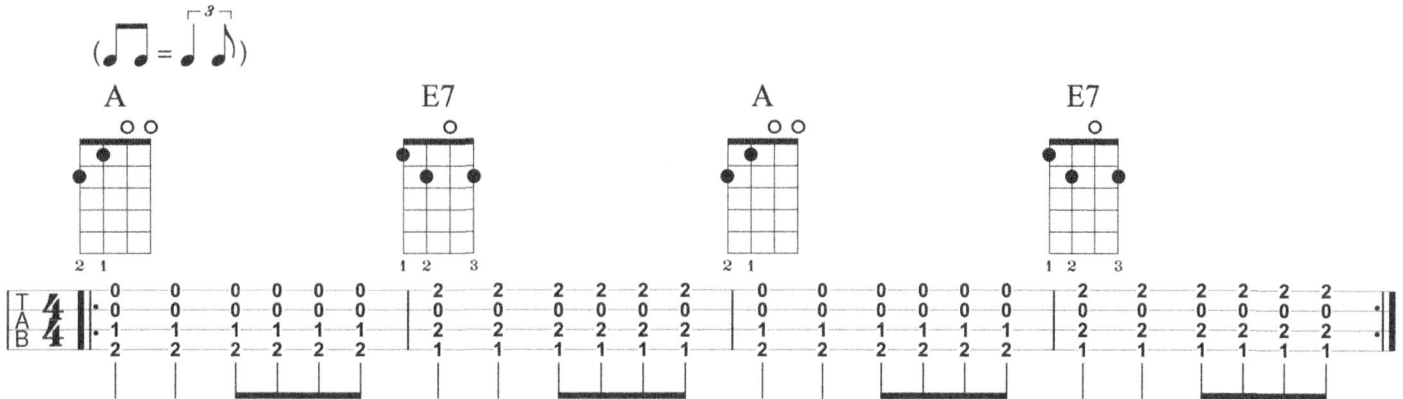

DAY 5

MAJOR CHORD (1:00–0:50)

The D major chord squeezes three notes into the space at the second fret on the bottom three strings, leaving the high A string to ring open. Because of this tight fit, it can be a bit tricky, and there are several ways you can fret the notes. Here, you'll use your middle finger on the 4th string, your index finger on the 3rd string, and your ring finger on the 2nd string. You could reverse your middle and index fingers, if you'd like, but because the D chord is played so often either before or after an A or A7 chord, the fingering here makes that change slightly easier. Some ukulele players even use their middle, ring, and pinky fingers on strings 4–2, respectively. Try them all and decide which works best for you.

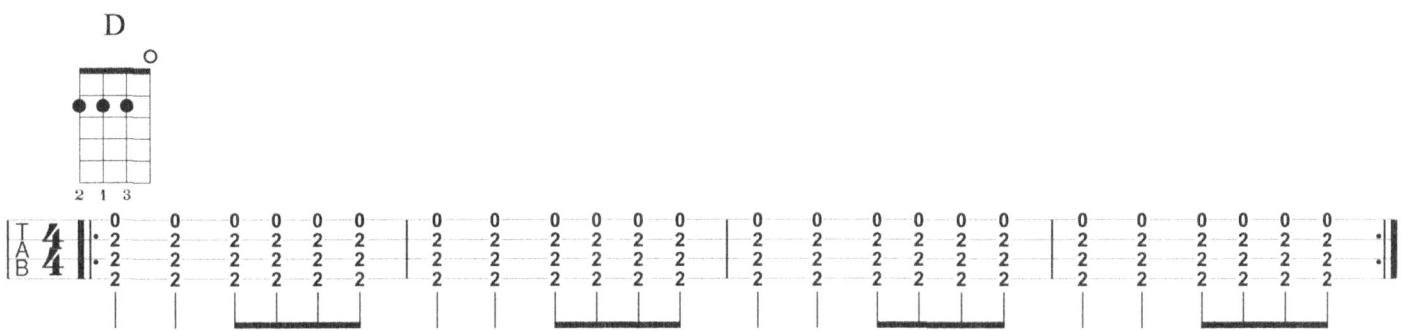

MINOR CHORD (0:50–0:40)

Though the Fm chord is not all that common in beginner ukulele songs, it's nonetheless a handy chord to know. Plus, it presents a slightly challenging chord shape and thus makes a good exercise for getting your fret hand's fingers properly arched to sound all the fretted notes cleanly while allowing the open C string to ring.

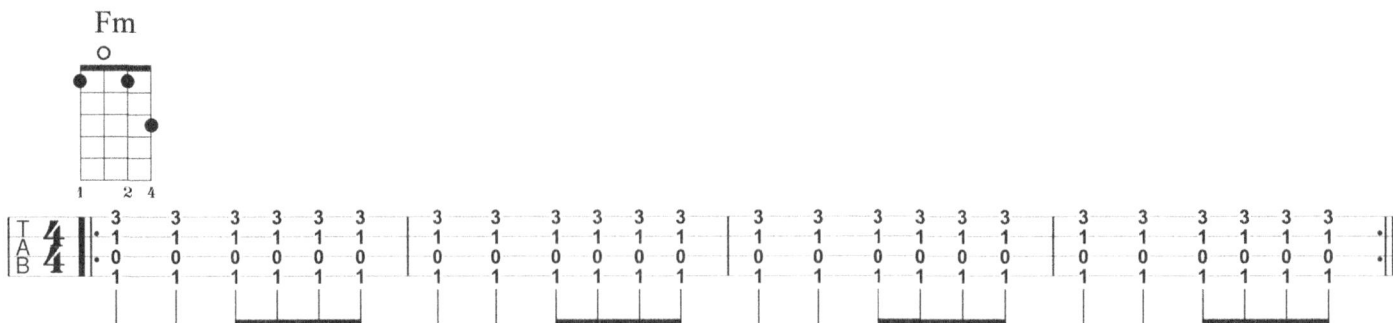

SEVENTH CHORD (0:40–0:30)

Like G7 is to C, and C7 is to F, the A7 chord is the V chord of D. To play A7, just place your fret hand's index finger at the first fret on the 3rd string, leaving all the others to ring open. Or, you can think of it as an A major chord, but without your middle finger on the 4th string.

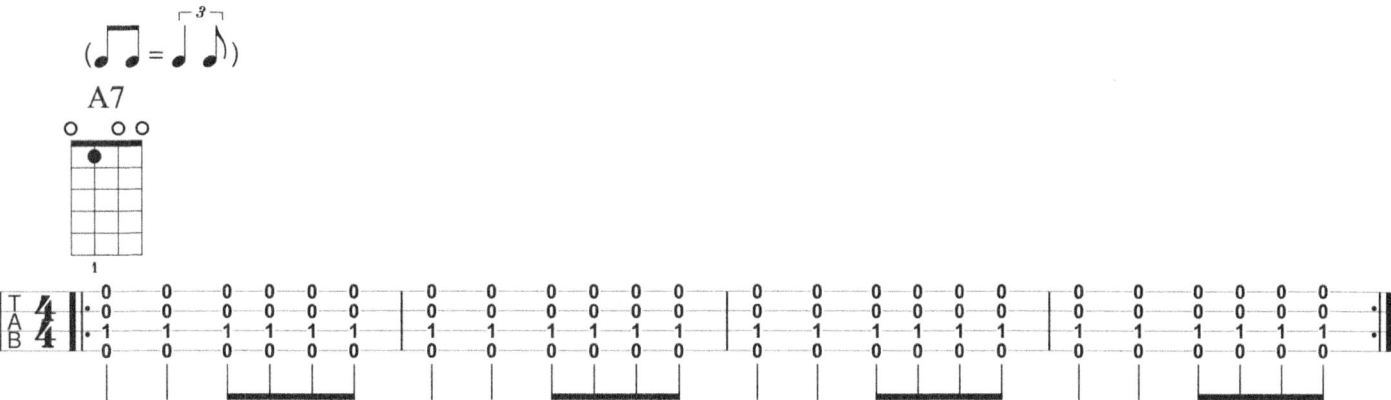

STRUM PATTERN (0:30–0:20)

Building on yesterday's strum pattern, this one adds yet another eighth-note pair, this time on beat 2. And just like yesterday's, this essential pattern is very common in pop and folk music.

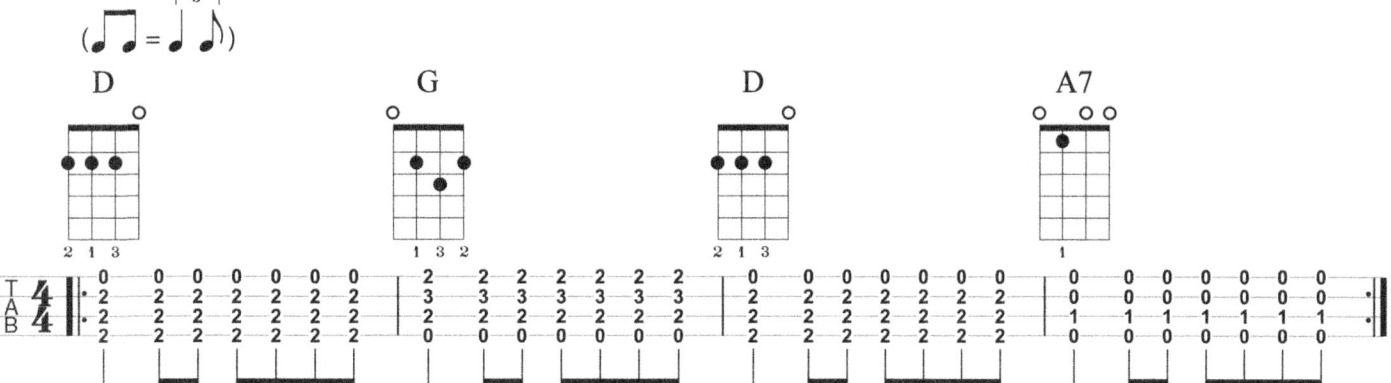

FINGERSTYLE PATTERN (0:20–0:10)

Borrowing from baseball parlance, we're going to throw you a little change-up for today's fingerstyle pattern. Here, you're going to ascend and descend all four strings in a quarter-note rhythm, but if you look closely, you'll see there are only three quarter notes in each measure. This is called 3/4 ("three-four") time and is most commonly associated with the waltz, though it's found in pop, country, folk, and spirituals, as well. This rhythm is counted thusly: "1–2–3, 1–2–3," etc.

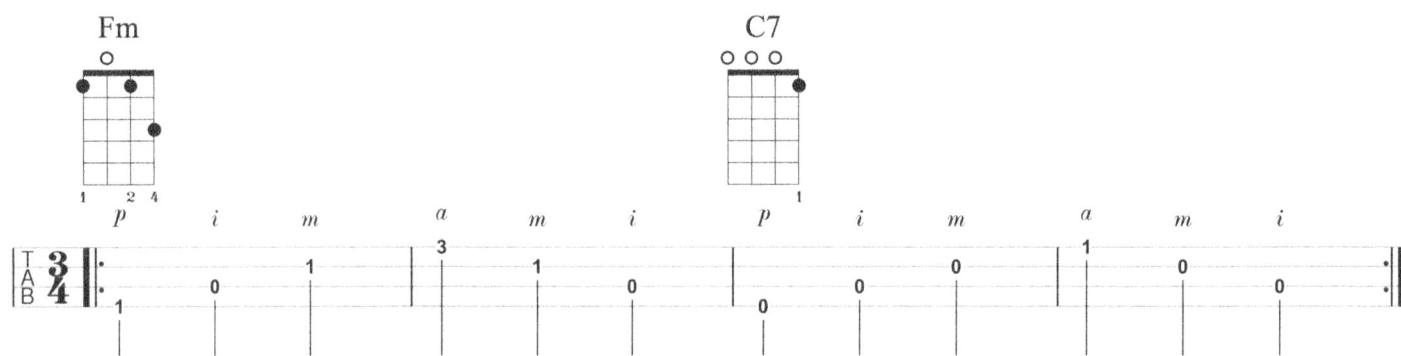

TECHNIQUE: CHEAT STRUM (0:10–0:00)

As you played through today's Strum Pattern exercise, you may have found that as your tempo increased, making the chord changes in time became more difficult. If so, don't feel bad—even seasoned pros hit this speed bump. But, they have a sneaky little trick to fly past it without a hitch in the rhythm—the *cheat strum*. All you have to do is lift all your fingers from the fretboard a half beat early—in this case, on the "and" of beat 4 in each measure—and strum all four strings open while you make the transition to the next chord. Try the progression from the Strum Pattern section again, which is shown below with the cheat strums added.

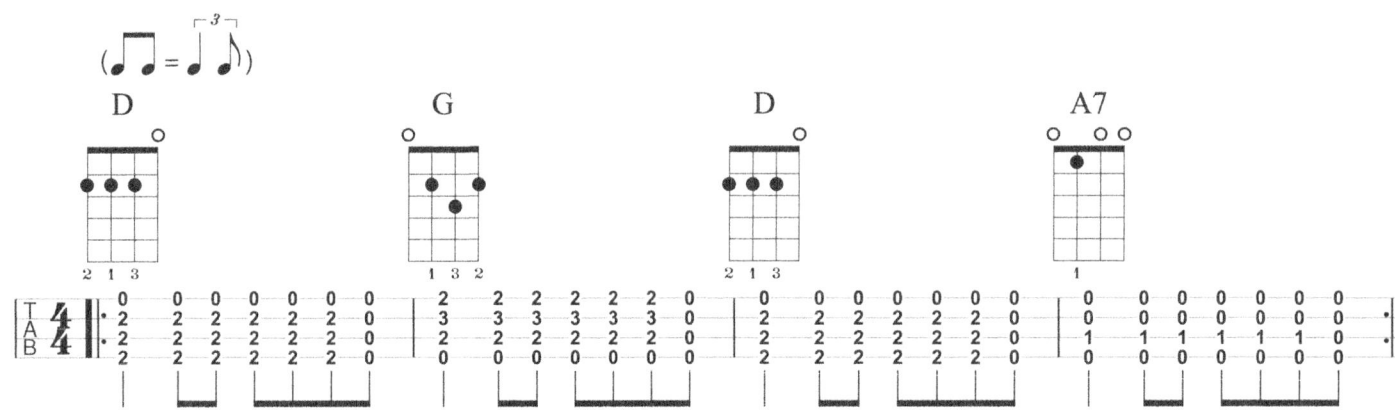

DAY 6

MAJOR CHORD (1:00–0:50)

It's time to kick things up a notch and introduce your first movable barre chord, B♭ (B-flat). But first, let's unpack all these new terms. Up until now, all the chords you've learned contained a ringing open string, so they can only be played in the shape and position you learned them. This new B♭ chord has fretted notes on all 4 strings, which means you can play it anywhere on the fretboard; thus, it's movable. Second, it's considered a *barre* chord because you have to "bar" your first finger across the top two strings to play two notes with one finger.

This movable shape is based on the A major chord you learned on Day 4; you just slide that A major shape up one fret and use your fret hand's index finger to cover strings 1–2. The root, which is the note for which the chord is named, is the note on the 1st string. So, if you move the shape up to 3rd position, you're playing a C major chord (because the note at fret 3 of the 1st string is C).

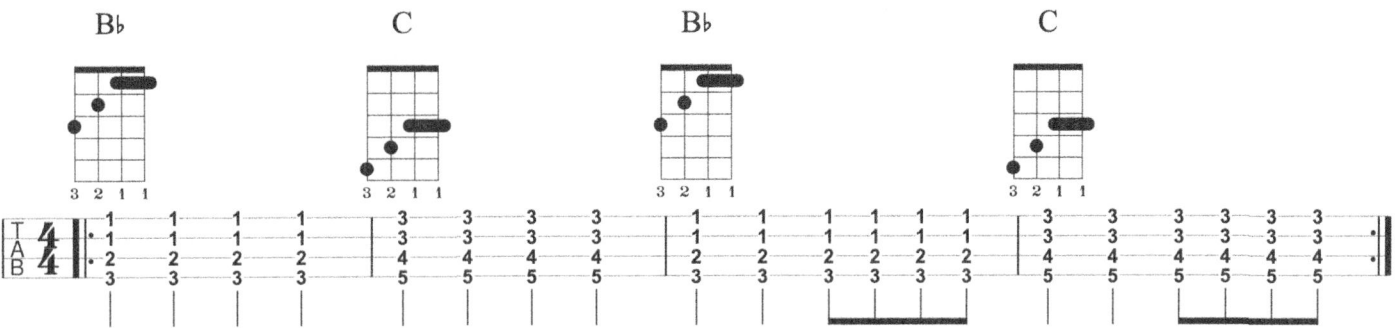

Music Theory Tip: If you're not familiar with *flats* or *sharps* in music, a flat *lowers* a pitch by one musical half step, or one fret on the ukulele; and a sharp *raises* a pitch by one musical half step, or one fret on the ukulele. For example, a B♭ chord is one half step, or one fret, lower than a B chord, and a C♯ note is one half step, or one fret, higher than a C note.

MINOR CHORD (0:50–0:40)

The B♭m chord is almost the same as the B♭ major chord, except the note on the 3rd string is lowered by a half step, which requires you to hold down, or barre, strings 3–1 with your index finger, as shown in the chord diagram. Like the B♭ major chord, the B♭m chord shape is movable, with its root note appearing on the 1st string.

In the following exercise, you'll strum both B♭m and Cm chords. If all four strings aren't ringing clearly, do a chord check and adjust your grip on the chord accordingly, but avoid over-squeezing the chord shape. Press down only enough so that the strings ring out clearly; too much pressure can lead to muscle fatigue, and even conditions like tendinitis, if done often enough.

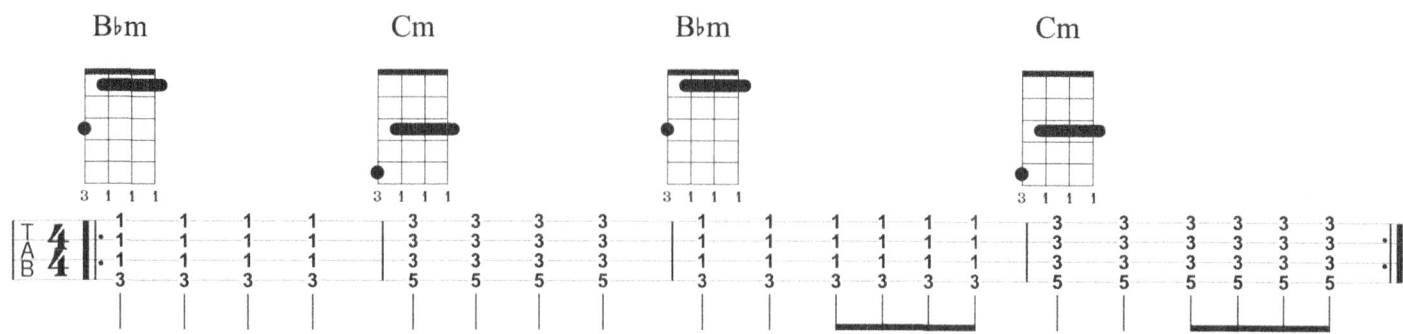

SEVENTH CHORD (0:40–0:30)

The V chord in the key of B♭ is F7; thus, the two are often heard together. The physical shape of this chord is the same as the Gm from Day 4, only shifted over one string set, so that now the 1st string rings open. You can also think of it as an F major chord, with your ring finger added on the 3rd fret of the 3rd string.

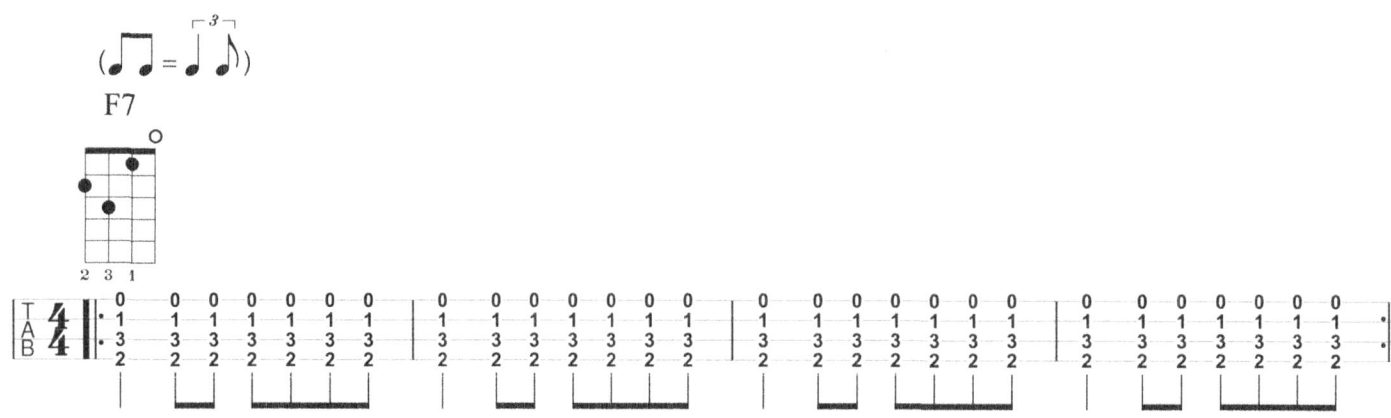

STRUM PATTERN (0:30–0:20)

Today's strum pattern is the same as yesterdays, except that it includes a tie between the "and" of beat 2 and the downbeat of beat 3. A tie, symbolized by a curved line, "connects" two notes or chords; that is, when you see a tie in the music, it means that you hold the note or chord for the total time duration of the two tied notes. For example, if you see a quarter note tied to an eighth note, you'd play the quarter note as indicated and then let that note or chord ring out for the duration of the quarter note plus the eighth note. So, in this strum pattern, you'll strum on the upbeat of beat 2, and then let the chord ring through beat 3, resuming the strum pattern on the upbeat of beat 3. Remember that you can use a *cheat strum*, if necessary.

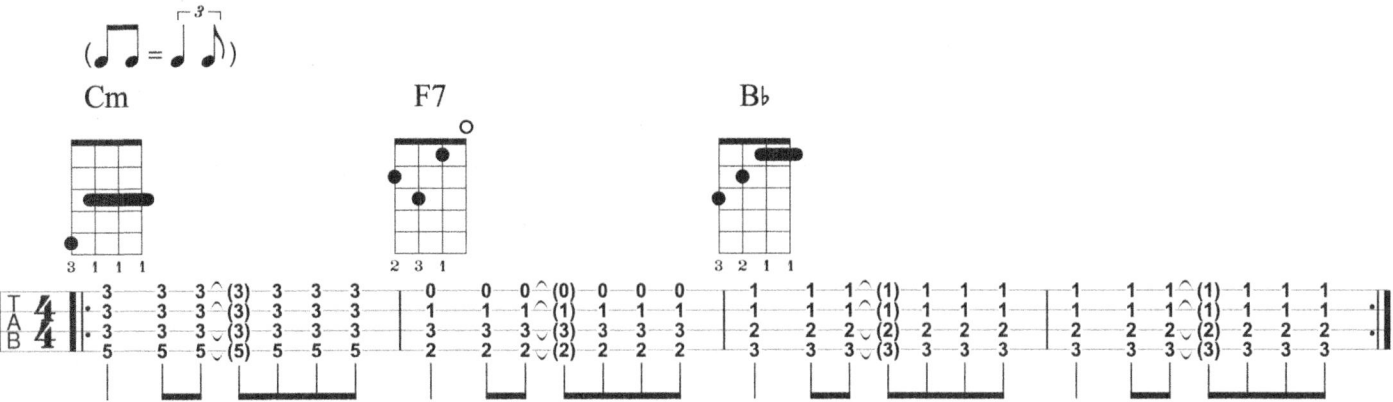

FINGERSTYLE PATTERN (0:20–0:10)

The fingerstyle pattern below returns to 4/4 time and features an ascending and descending picking pattern, with an added bonus at the end. Specifically, you'll play *pima* in measure 1, followed by *miam* in measure 2. This pattern is then repeated in measures 3–4.

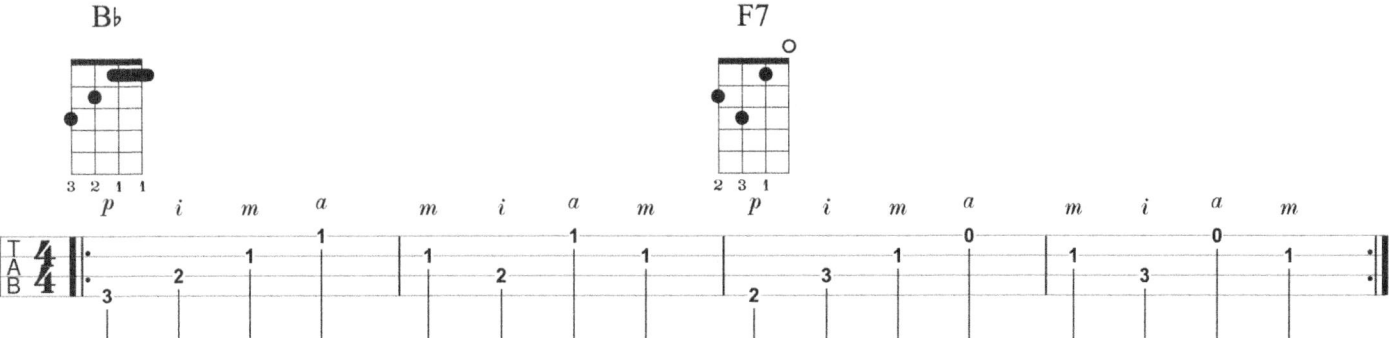

27

TECHNIQUE: SINGLE-STRING MAJOR SCALE (0:10–0:00)

Today, you're going to revisit the major scale, only this time, you're going to play it all on one string. This will serve two purposes: first, it will clearly illustrate how a major scale is constructed, and second, it will give you a feel for playing single notes higher up on the neck.

To begin, the major scale is constructed of seven notes with a specific pattern of whole- (two frets) and half-step (one fret) intervals: W–W–H–W–W–W–H. So, for example, if you start on the open A (1st) string, the next note is a whole step, or two frets, away, which is B on the 2nd fret. Then another whole step brings you to C♯ on the 4th fret. A half step takes you to D on the 5th fret, then three straight whole steps to E, F♯, and G♯ (frets 7, 9, 11, respectively), followed by a half step to bring you back to the root, A, at the 12th fret. Use your thumb to pluck each note. Try the suggested fingering for your fret hand, but experiment if have trouble. Once you're comfortable with the A major scale on the 1st string, try the E (2nd string), C (3rd string), and G (4th string) major scales, using this same intervallic pattern.

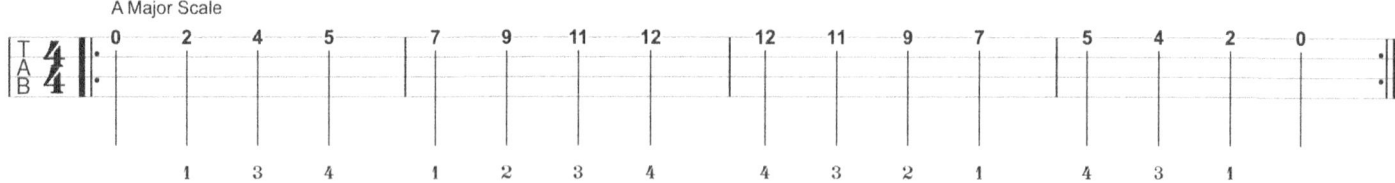

DAY 7 – WEEK 1 REVIEW: PUTTING IT ALL TOGETHER

"AURA LEE" CHORDS (1:00–0:30)

It's Day 7—the end of your first week of playing the ukulele, and you've learned *a lot*—enough, in fact, to play the traditional folk song "Aura Lee," which basically serves as the chords and melody to "Love Me Tender" by Elvis Presley. This arrangement is in the key of F and features quite a few of the chords you learned this week. It's presented here with simple quarter and eighth notes. You can play it as written the first time, but then try using some of the strum patterns you learned this week, or even a fingerstyle pattern.

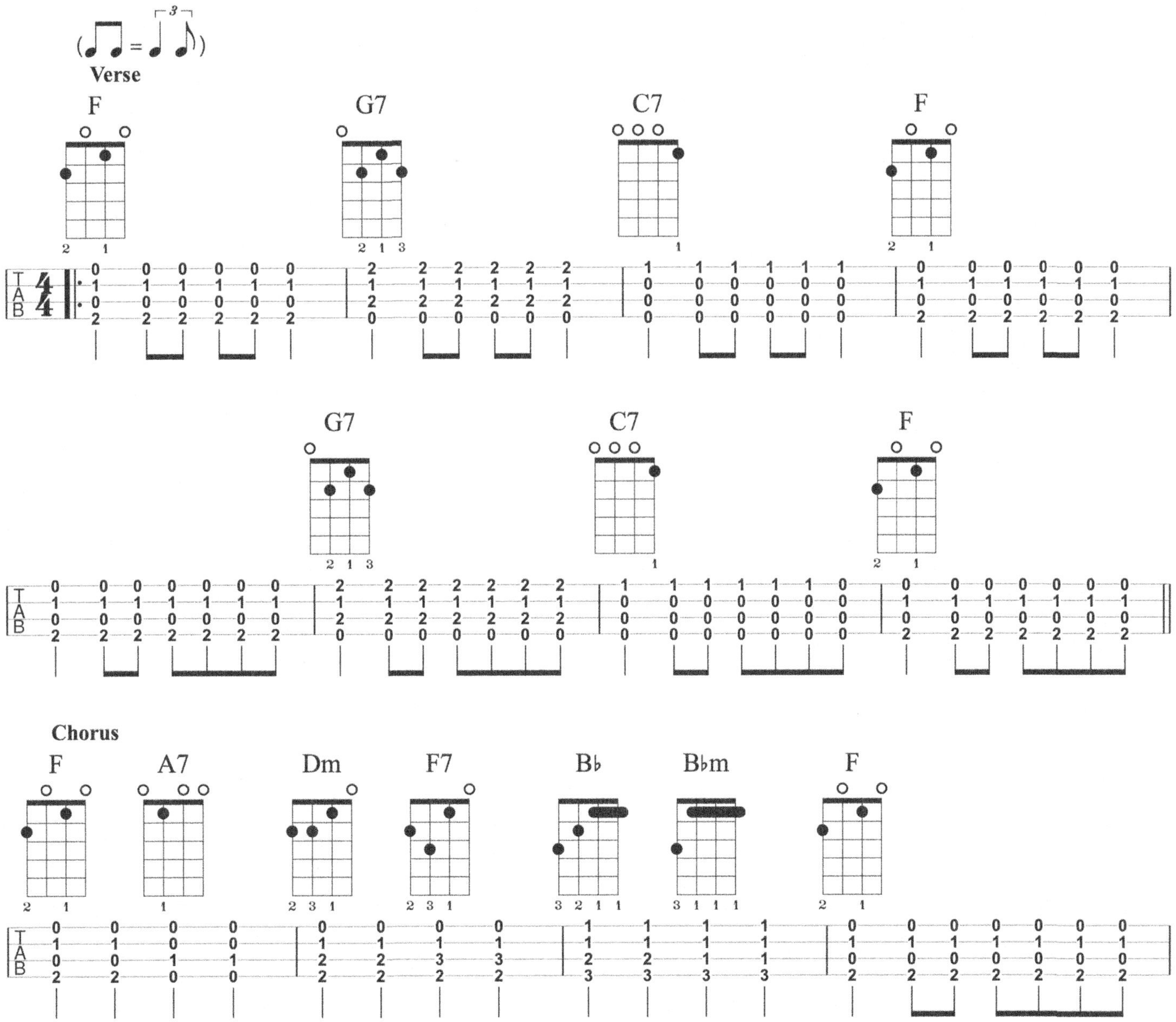

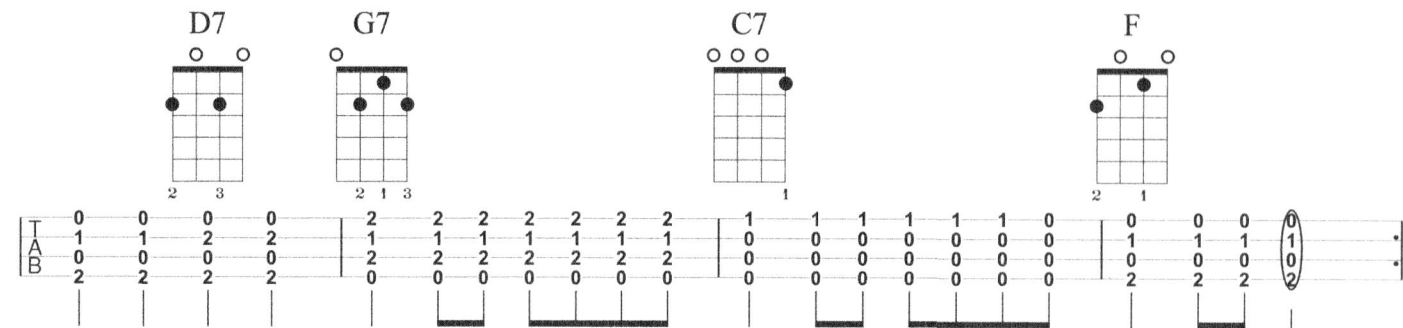

"AURA LEE" MELODY (0:30–0:00)

Now that you've strummed the chords to "Aura Lee," it's time to put your single-note plucking to the test and play the melody. Practice it solo a few times until you feel that you've got a good handle on it, using the audio track as a guide. Once you can play along with the audio track, go back to the previous example and play the melody over the audio of the "Aura Lee" chords.

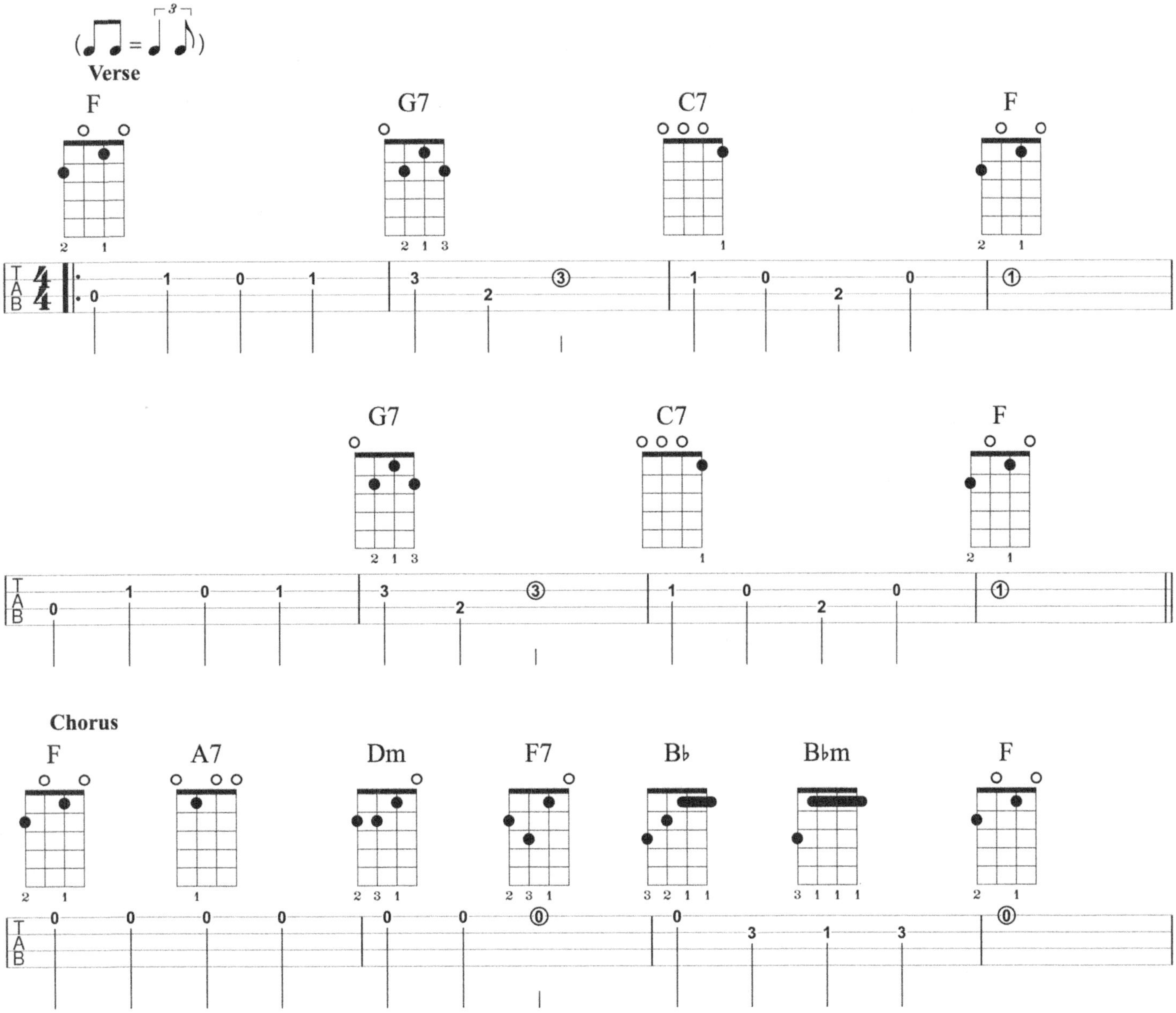

31

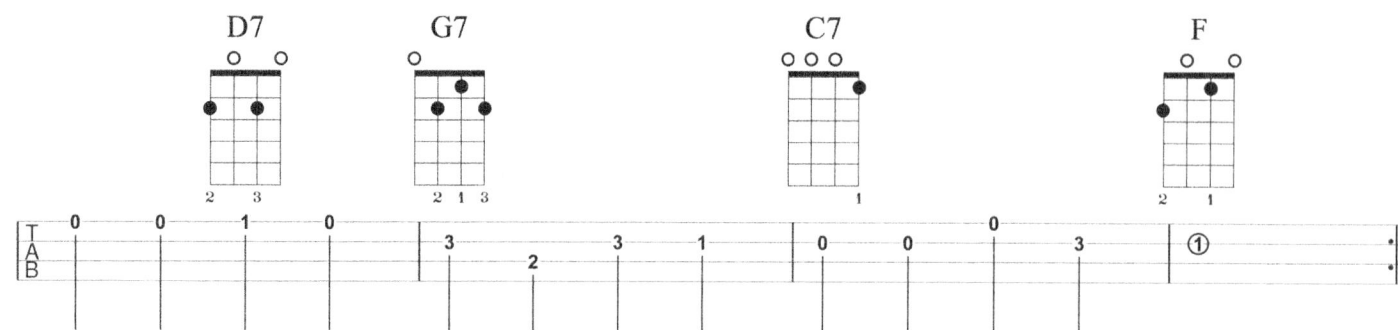

DAY 8

MAJOR CHORD (1:00–0:50)

You learned almost all of the most important major and minor chords for ukulele last week, except for one—E major. There are a few ways to play a basic E major chord on the ukulele. Two are not very "finger-friendly," but the third is not only fairly easy but also movable and, when played two frets lower, is an excellent alternative shape for D major. The shape below requires you to play strings 4–2 with an index-finger barre, while your pinky grabs the note on string 1.

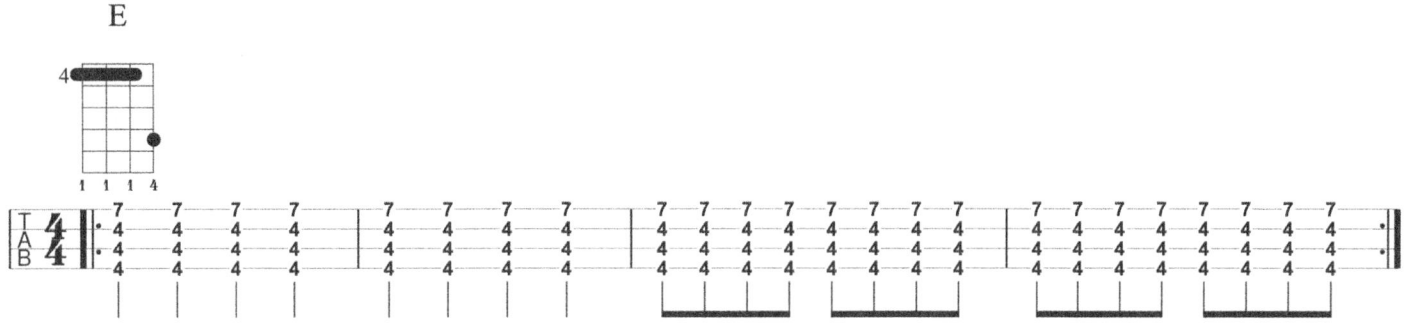

MINOR CHORD (0:50–0:40)

The movable E minor chord shown here is the same as the open version you learned on Day 3, but instead of using the open 4th string, this version includes the fretted B note at the 4th fret on string 4; therefore, this shape requires a slightly different fingering than the open version: here, fret that 4th-fret B with your ring finger and the 4th-fret E (the chord's root) on the 3rd string with your pinky finger.

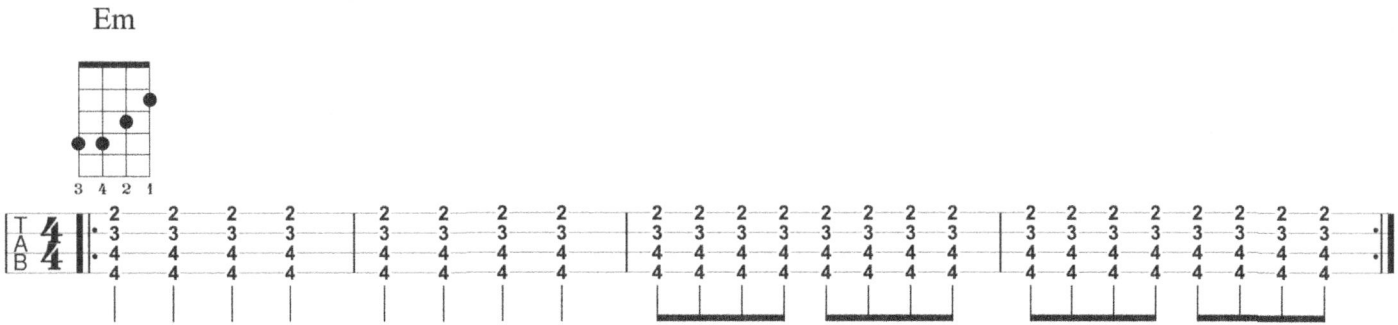

SEVENTH CHORD (0:40–0:30)

On Day 6, you learned the movable B♭ major and B♭ minor chord shapes, which, when played at the 2nd fret, are B and Bm, respectively. Likewise, the root of today's seventh chord, B7, is located at the 2nd fret on the 1st string. To play it, lay your index finger across all four strings at the 2nd fret to form a barre, then place your middle finger on the 3rd string at the 3rd fret and strum all four strings. Note that B7 is the V chord of E major.

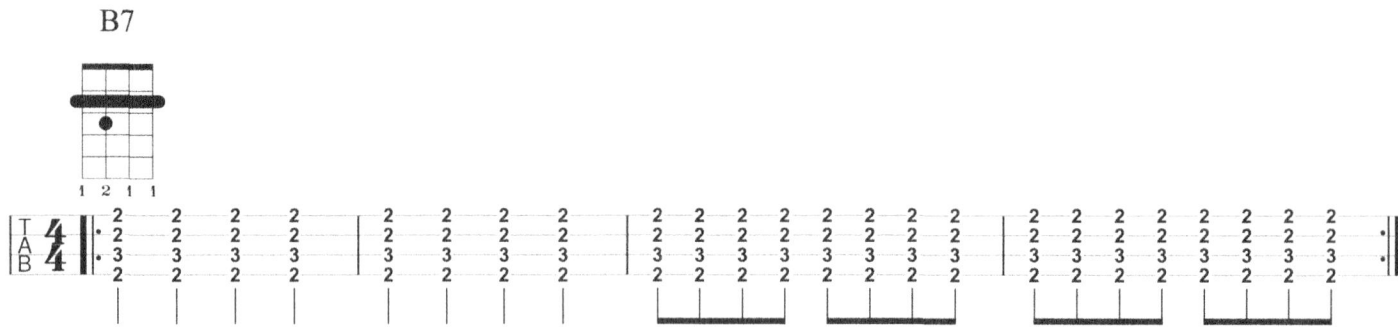

STRUM PATTERN (0:30–0:20)

This strum pattern is an essential one—a nonstop eighth-note rhythm. It's very straightforward, but work to maintain a steady rhythm throughout, whether playing it in a straight rhythm or in a shuffle, as shown here, as it's very easy to unintentionally speed up.

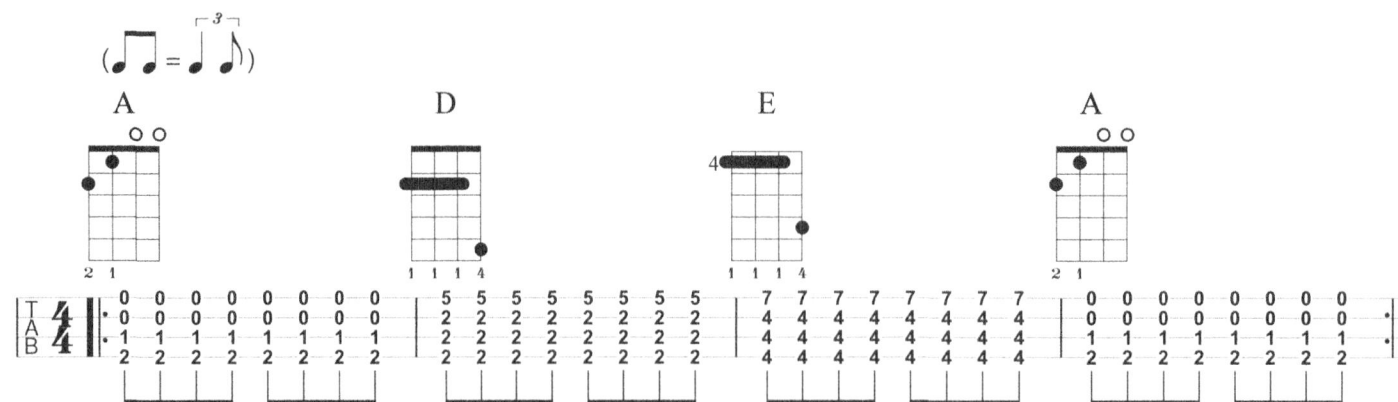

34

FINGERSTYLE PATTERN (0:20–0:10)

Because the 4th string on the ukulele is tuned an octave higher than what you find on, say, a guitar or four-string banjo, picking the strings from 4–1 does not result in the pitch going from low to high. So, if you want to play a chord fingerstyle, with the notes sounding from low to high, you need to start your pattern on the *3rd* string. Though it won't *always* result in a low-to-high orientation, this pattern will prove very useful as you learn to play your favorite songs.

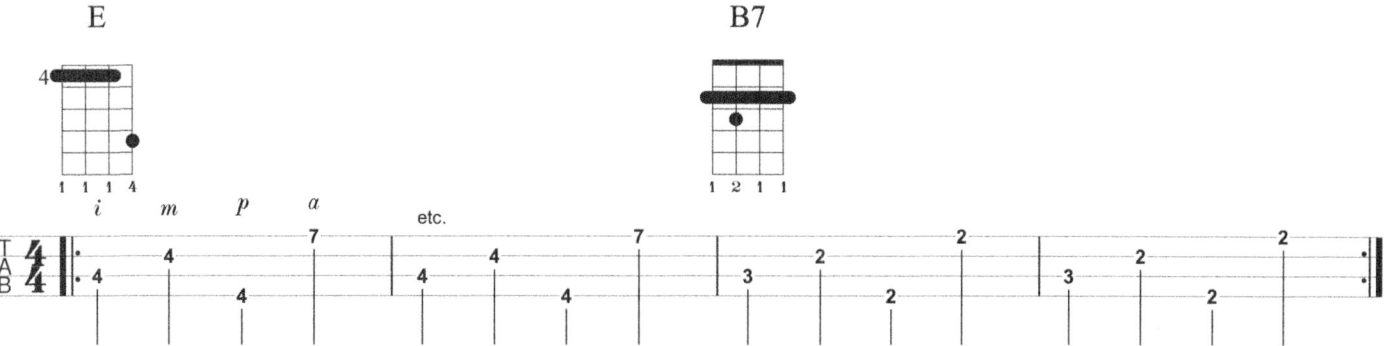

TECHNIQUE: INDEX-FINGER STRUM (0:10–0:00)

Up to this point, you've been strumming chords with your thumb. Now it's time to learn the more versatile index-finger strum. To perform this technique, first form a loose "gun" shape with your right hand; that is, start with your hand in a loose fist, stick your index finger straight out, extend your thumb upward, and leave the remaining three fingers curled inward. Now, turn your hand so that your index finger is pointing downward, perpendicular to the strings, positioned between where the neck joins the body and the edge of the sound hole. Then, rotate your wrist so that your index finger strums in an up-and-down motion. Again, keep everything loose and relaxed. If you have time, go back and practice all of today's examples with the index-finger strum.

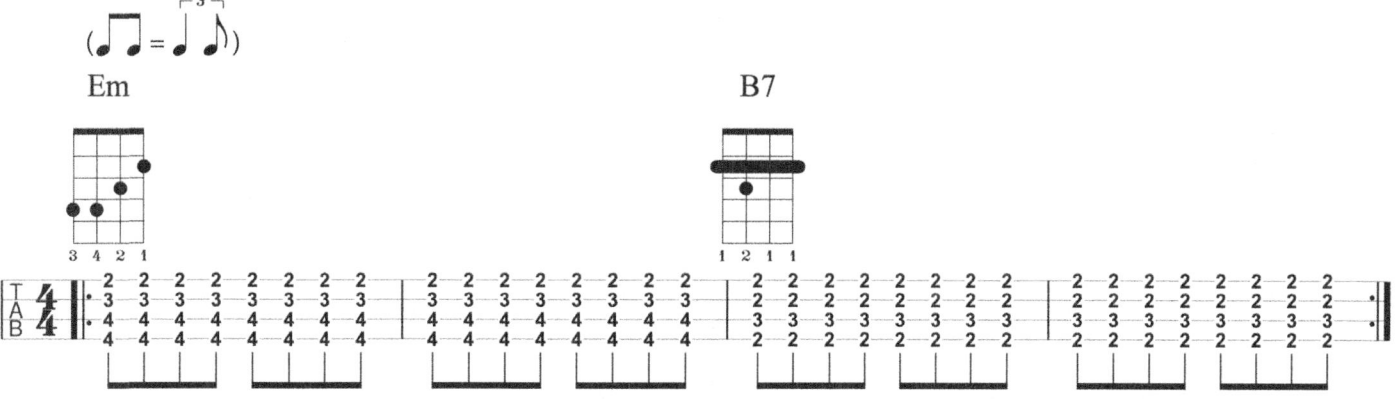

DAY 9

MAJOR CHORD (1:00–0:50)

This new movable major chord is a version of the open G chord you learned on Day 3. In fact, you can play it with the exact same fingering but then adding your pinky finger to the 4th string at the 4th fret. Alternatively, you can treat it like a barre chord, laying your index finger across all four strings at the 2nd fret, then place your ring finger on the 4th string at the 4th fret and your middle finger on the 2nd string at the 3rd fret. Try both and use whichever is more comfortable. The root of this movable chord is found on the 2nd string, 3rd fret.

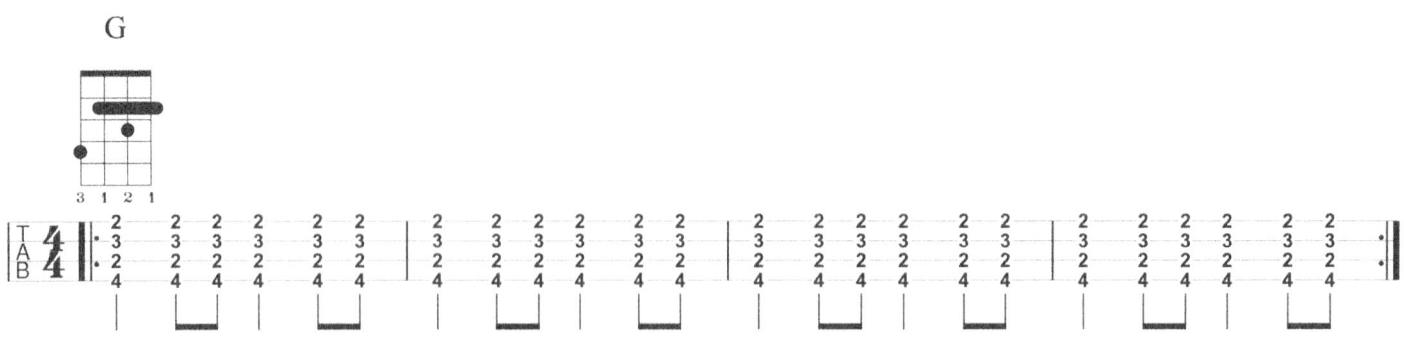

MINOR CHORD (0:50–0:40)

Today's movable minor chord shape is a *minor 7th* chord. It's basically the same as the 7th chords you've been playing, except that it contains a flatted 3rd interval. If you compare the Bm7 shape in the example below to the B7 chord you learned yesterday, you'll see that the note on the 3rd string has been lowered one fret, so now you just barre across all four strings with your fret hand's index finger. Make sure all four strings ring clearly.

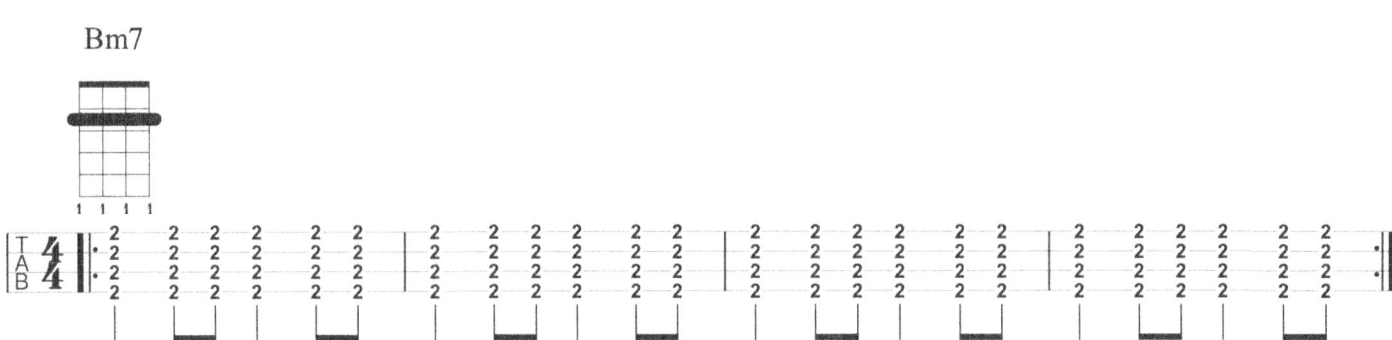

SEVENTH CHORD (0:40–0:30) 🔊

Last week, you learned the open D7 chord. Today, you're going to learn the movable D7 chord, which is just as commonly used. To play this one, lay your index finger across strings 4–2 at the 2nd fret to form a barre, then add your middle finger to the 1st string at the 3rd fret.

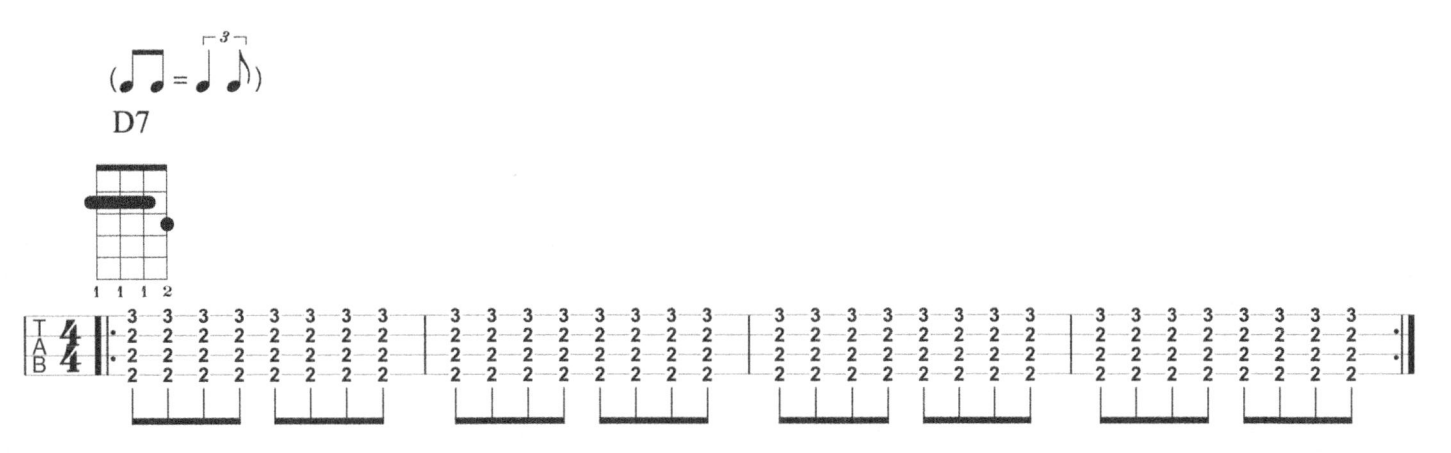

STRUM PATTERN (0:30–0:20) 🔊

Today's strum pattern features a "choked" strum on beat 1 of each measure. In measures 1 and 2 of the example below, it's shown using an eighth-note strum on the downbeat, followed by an eighth-note rest on the upbeat, just to help you understand the basic "time" of the strum. More accurately, this is called a *staccato* strum, which means you mute the chord immediately after strumming it. This is indicated by a small dot above the chord in the tab, as shown in measures 3 and 4. Listen to the accompanying audio to hear how it should sound.

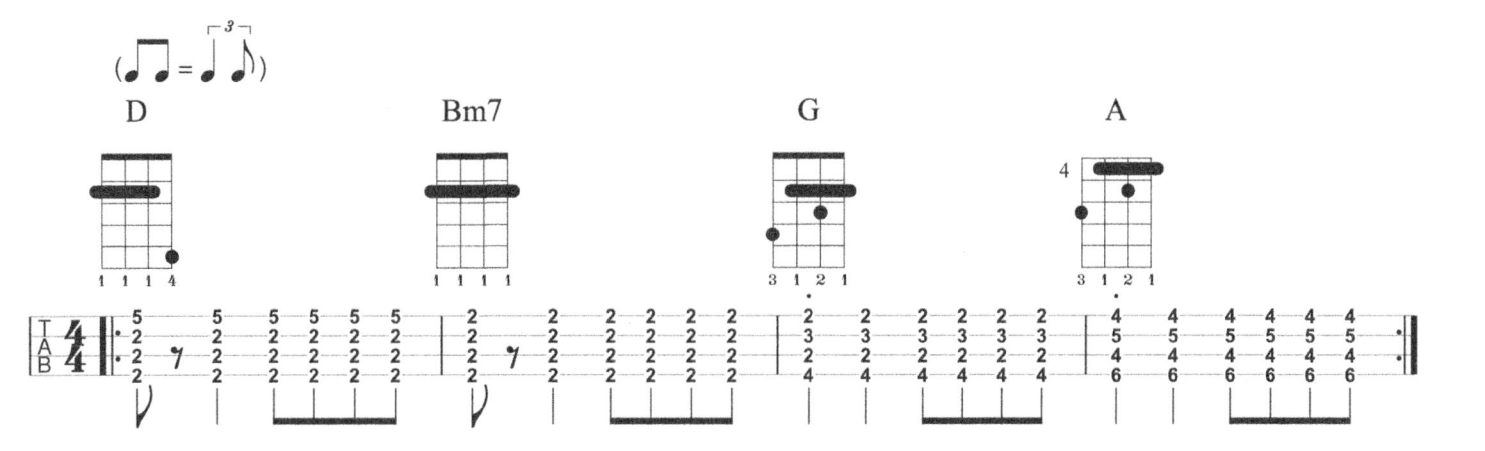

FINGERSTYLE PATTERN (0:20–0:10) 🔊

The fingerstyle pattern shown below is the descending version of the arpeggio you learned yesterday. Use the *apmi* pattern for your picking hand, starting very slowly so that you can make the chord changes while staying in time.

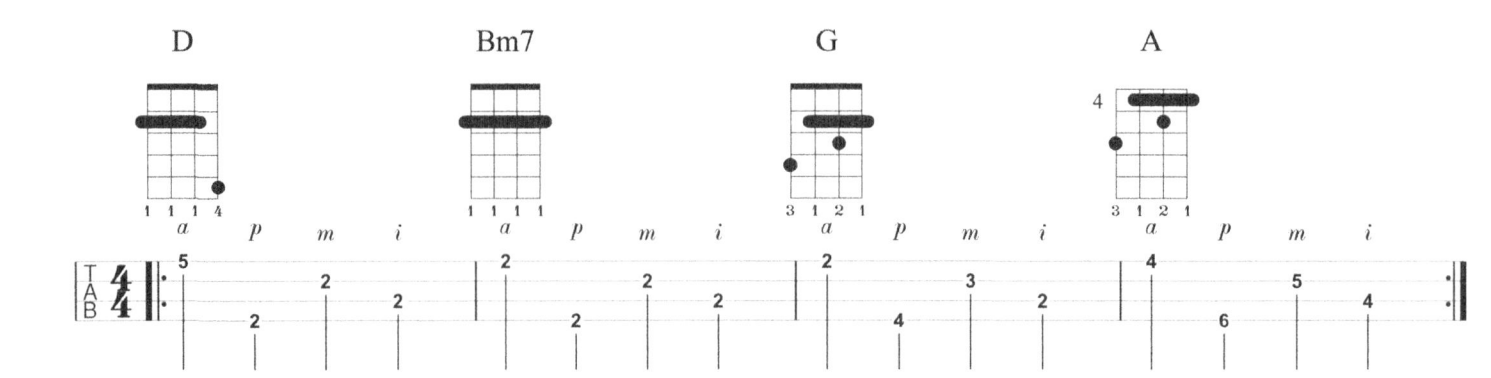

TECHNIQUE: FRET-HAND MUTED STRUM (0:10–0:00) 🔊

The muted-strum technique is absolutely essential to playing the ukulele. Just as the name implies, you simply strum all four strings of the ukulele while lightly touching them with your fret hand so that no notes ring out; instead, you get a percussive "scratch."

In practice, all you need to do is lift your fret-hand fingers from whatever chord shape you're playing just enough so that the uke's strings are no longer making contact with the metal fret wires. But be sure to keep your fingers over their correct positions for the chord. Doing so will allow you to produce the muted strum quickly and then return to the fretted chord equally fast without missing a beat. Note that you'll most often hear these muted strums on beats 2 and 4, as they are meant to imitate the snare drum.

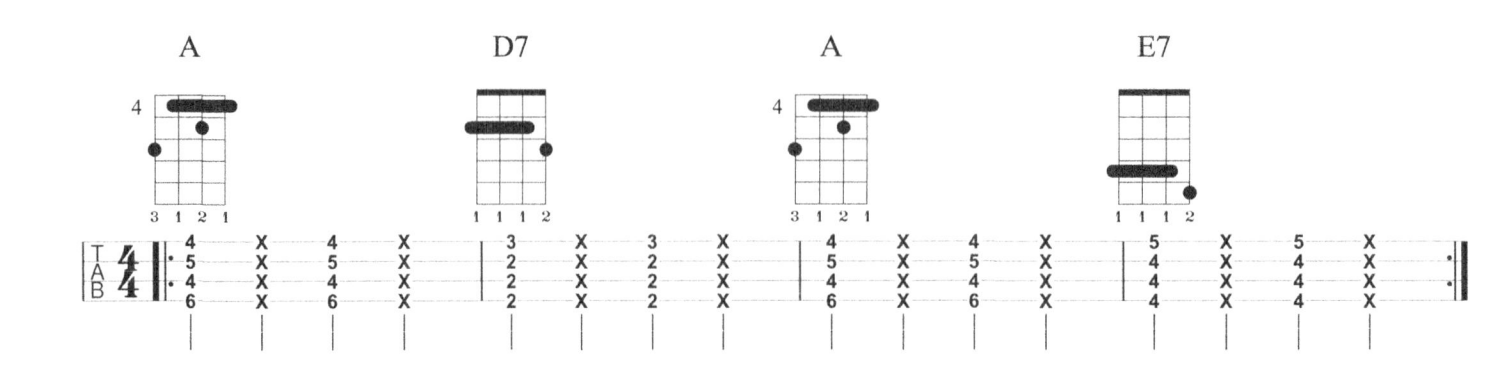

DAY 10

MAJOR CHORD (1:00–0:50) 🔊

For today's movable chord exercise, let's revisit the G major chord from Day 2. You're going to play the exact same chord, only the 4th string should be muted with the side of your fret hand's index finger, which is fretting the 3rd string. Then, try to strum only the top three strings.

Next, slide that same shape up five frets to play an C major chord, and then up two more frets to play D major. Once you're comfortable with the shapes, add the muted strums on beats 2 and 4 in each measure, playing the exercise as written. Keep in mind that the root note for this shape is on the 2nd string. With that in mind, try moving the chord around however you want, using your ear as your guide.

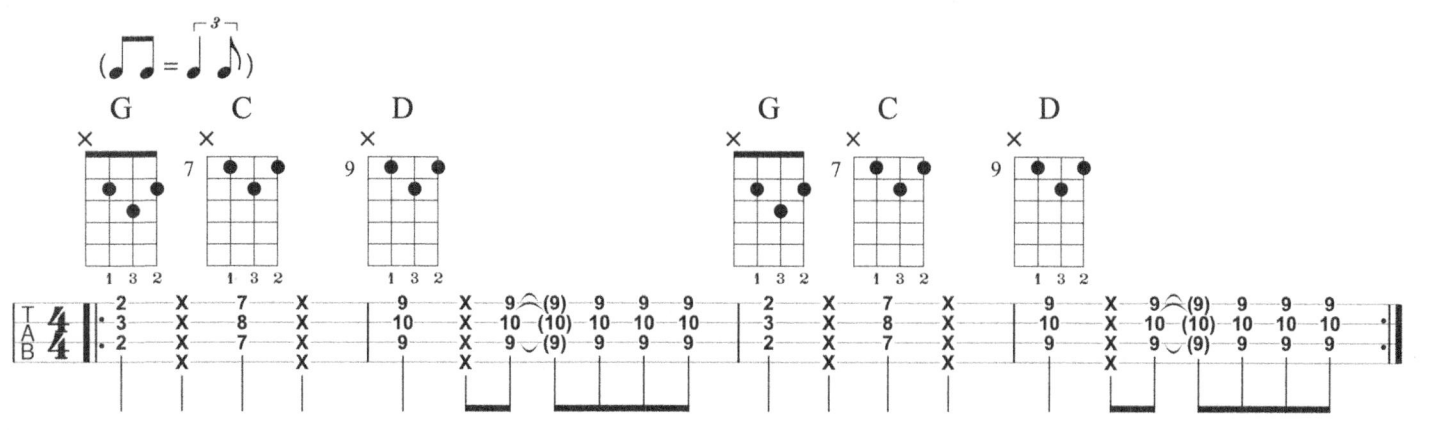

MINOR CHORD (0:50–0:40) 🔊

Now let's take a look at the movable G minor chord shape. It's the same as the Gm chord you learned on Day 4, but like its sister major chord above, you only play the top three strings, muting the 4th string as necessary. Also like the major shape, feel free to move this one around, using your ear to determine what you like and don't like.

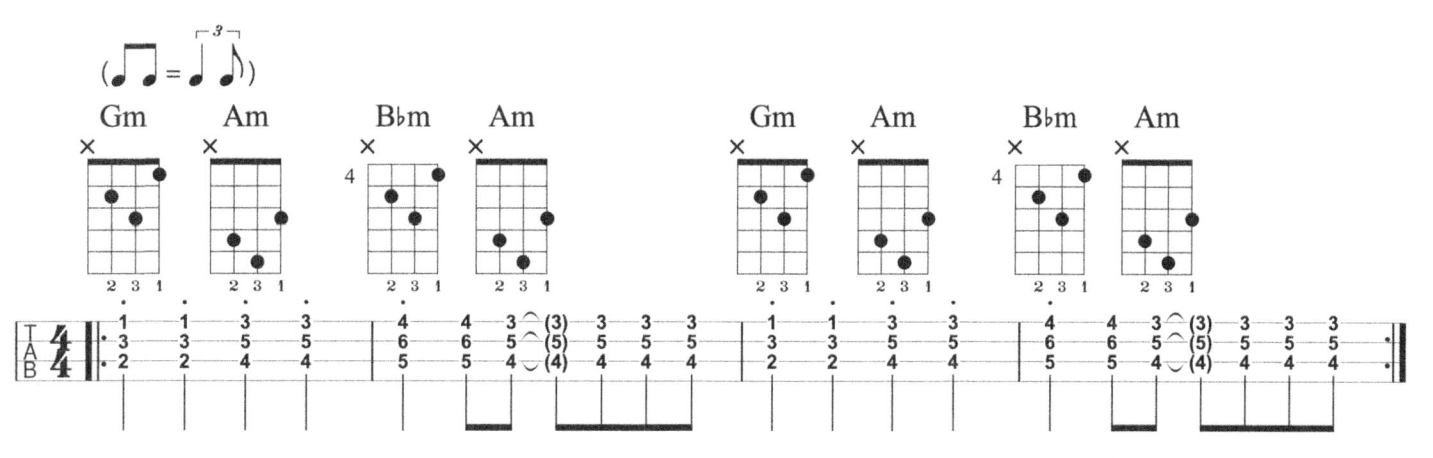

SEVENTH CHORD (0:40–0:30)

Sticking with the various "G shapes," this exercise features the open G7 chord shape moving *chromatically*, or one fret at a time, down the neck for an old-time bluesy sound. Remember to play only the top three strings when moving this shape around.

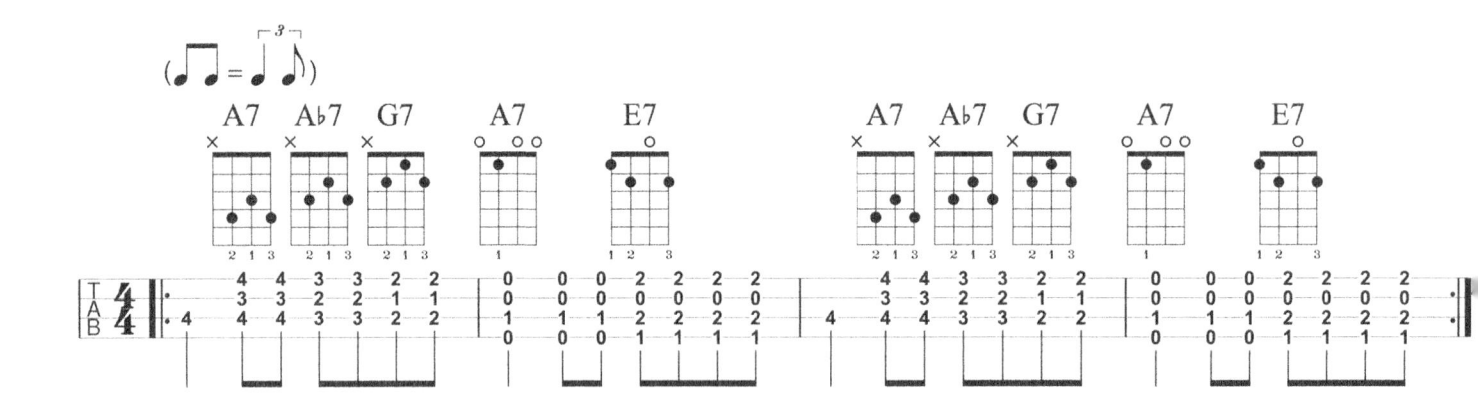

STRUM PATTERN (0:30–0:20)

Today's strum pattern is your introduction to 16th notes. Whereas eighth notes are the equivalent of splitting a quarter note in two, 16th notes are the result of splitting a quarter note into four equal parts. You won't often find yourself playing four 16th notes on every beat of a measure. More typically, you'll hear them used for just a couple of beats, as below, or on partial beats (see tomorrow's pattern).

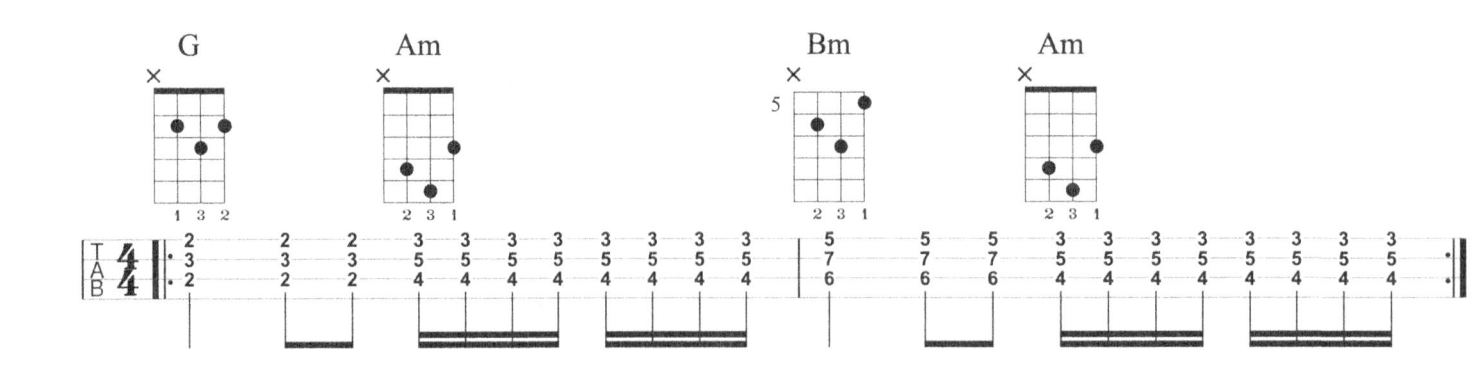

CHORD PROGRESSION: I–IV–I–V (0:20–0:10) 🔊

At this point in your journey to becoming a ukulele player, it's important to start learning chord progressions commonly used in popular music. Understanding and recognizing how various chords "fit together" will help tremendously when learning how to play your favorite songs. To do so, however, you'll need a quick music theory lesson.

On Day 6, you learned how to construct a major scale by using a series of whole- and half-step intervals. Using C as our root, the C major scale is spelled C–D–E–F–G–A–B. Now, we use the major scale to determine what chords belong in any given chord family by assigning each of those notes a number, from 1–7. Notes 1, 4, and 5 are the roots of the *major* chords in each key and are denoted with uppercase Roman numerals (I, IV, V). Notes 2, 3, and 6 are minor chords denoted with lowercase Roman numerals (ii, iii, vi). And note 7 is the root of the diminished chord (which you'll learn on Day 13) denoted with a lowercase Roman numeral and a small circle (vii°).

Armed with that knowledge, you can describe almost any chord progressions by using the Roman numerals. For example, your first—and arguably the most popular—chord progression is the I–IV–I–V, which, in the key of C, is C–F–C–G, as shown below. You'll hear this progression in timeless pop songs like "Brown-Eyed Girl," "Crazy Little Thing Called Love," and "You Are My Sunshine."

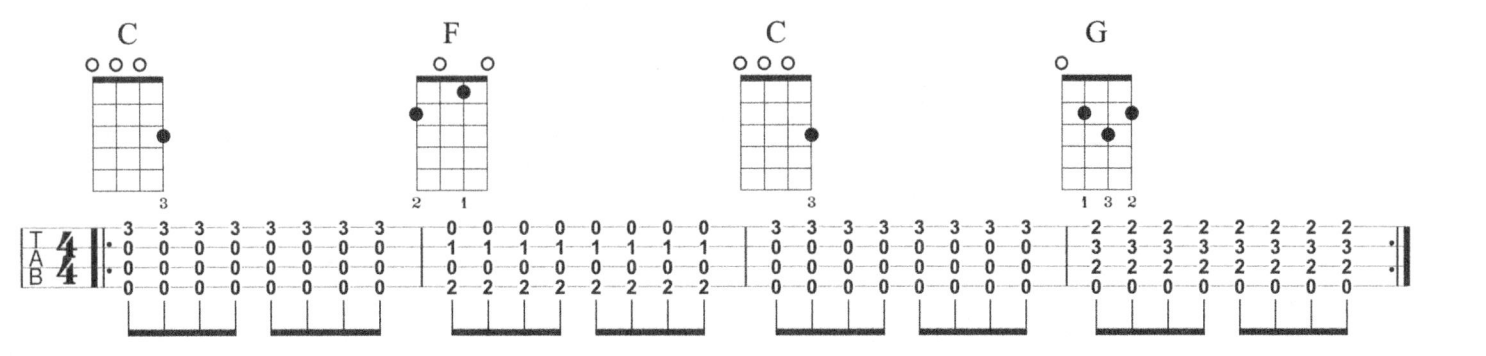

TECHNIQUE: STRUM-HAND MUTE (0:10–0:00) 🔊

Yesterday, you learned how to perform a muted strum by lifting your fingers from the fretted notes while still touching the strings. Although it's an effective and essential technique, it's not ideal when muting chords that contain open strings. This is where the strum-hand mute comes in. To perform a strum-hand mute, you'll attack the strings with your index finger as in a normal strum, but at the same time, you'll place the heel of your strum hand's palm against all four strings, thereby effectively muting them. Use the chord progression from the previous example, C–F–C–G (I–IV–I–V), to give it a try.

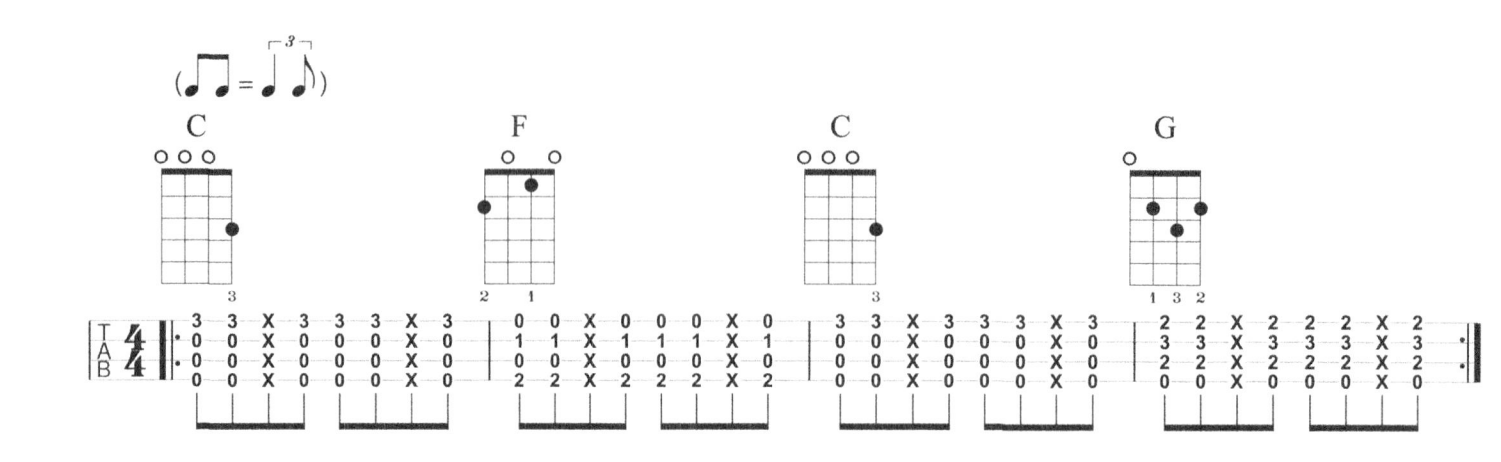

DAY 11

MAJOR CHORD (1:00–0:50) 🔊

For today's major chord, you're going to learn the jazzy *major 7th* chord, which is just like a regular 7th chord, except the 7th degree is moved up one fret. In the example below, you'll play both the open-position Cmaj7 chord and the movable shape—in this case, Dmaj7. You should recognize that the open-position shape is the same as a C7 chord, but with the fretted note at the 2nd fret, rather than the 1st. Typically, you'll use your middle finger to fret that note; however, since the example also teaches the movable version of this major 7th chord, where that 1st-string note is fretted with the ring finger, it's perfectly fine to use your ring finger on the open version, as well, to make the chord change easier.

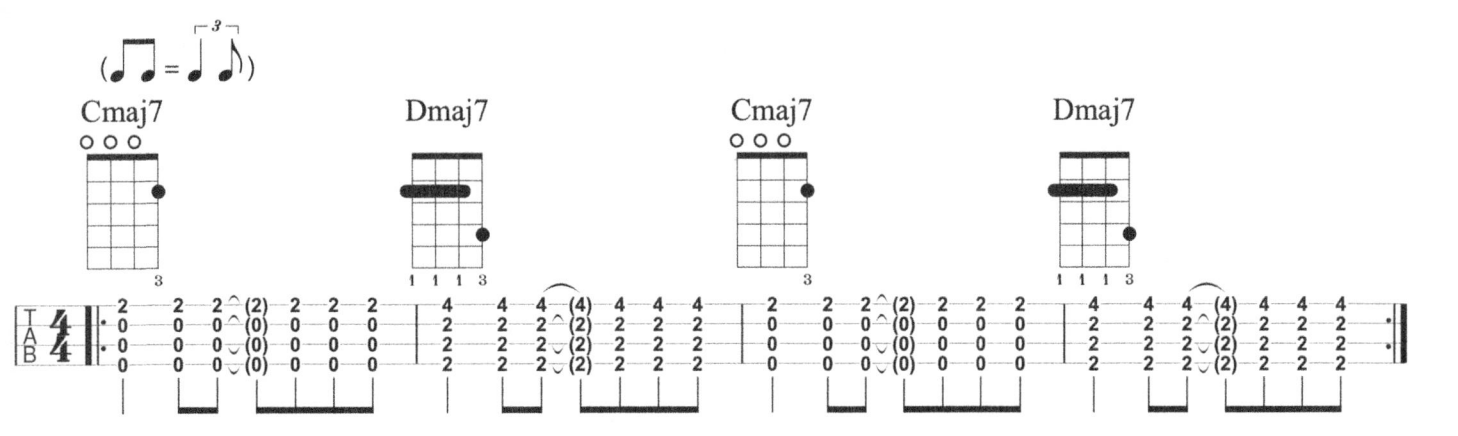

MINOR CHORD (0:50–0:40) 🔊

Based on the open Dm chord from Day 2, this minor 7th chord shape simply adds the pinky to the 1st string, thus making it a movable version with the root on the 3rd string.

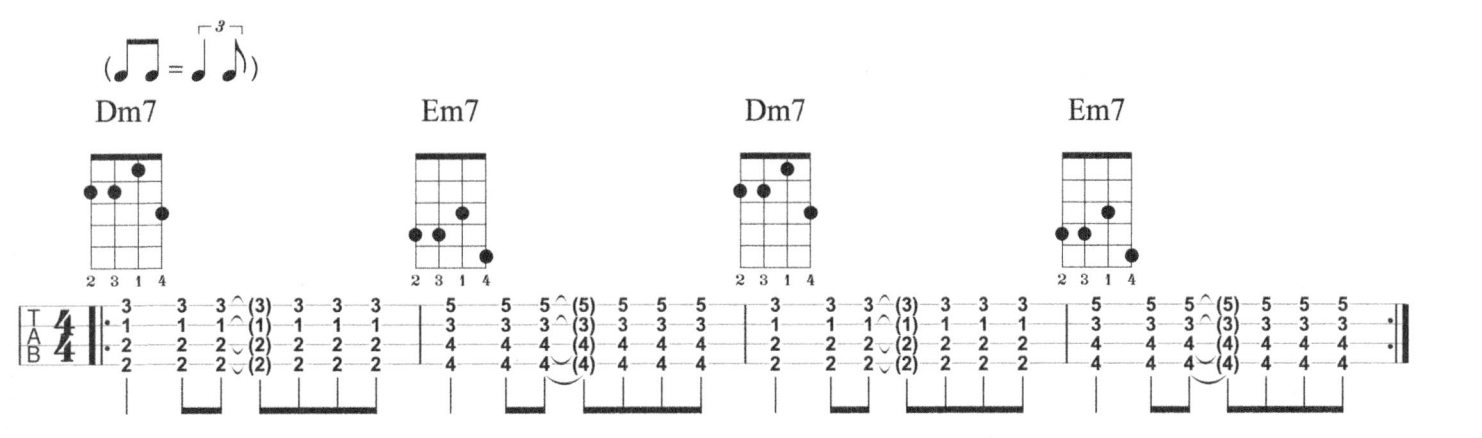

STRUM PATTERN (0:40–0:30) 🔊

The strum pattern shown below contains plenty of 16th notes, but its main feature is the tie that connects the final 16th note of beat 2 to the first 16th note of beat 3. On paper, or even counting it in your head, the pattern can be a bit intimidating, but it's an incredibly common strum pattern in popular music. Listen to the accompanying audio to get a feel for it.

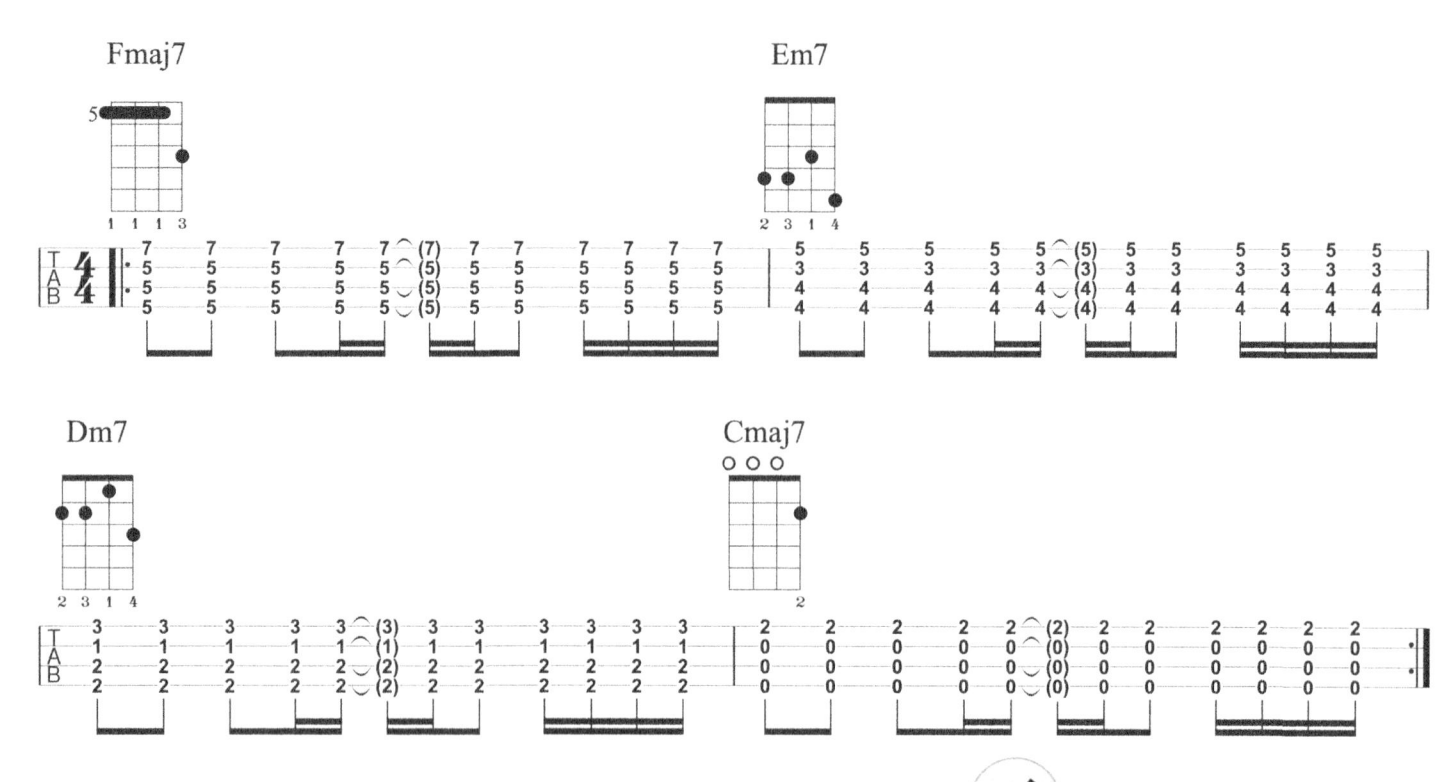

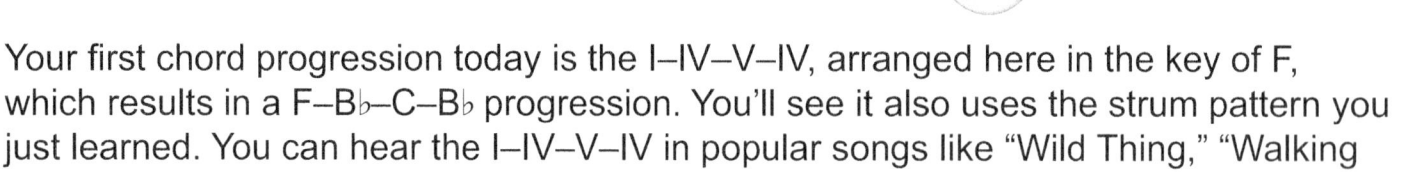

CHORD PROGRESSION: I–IV–V–IV (0:30–0:20) 🔊

Your first chord progression today is the I–IV–V–IV, arranged here in the key of F, which results in a F–B♭–C–B♭ progression. You'll see it also uses the strum pattern you just learned. You can hear the I–IV–V–IV in popular songs like "Wild Thing," "Walking on Sunshine," and "Louie, Louie."

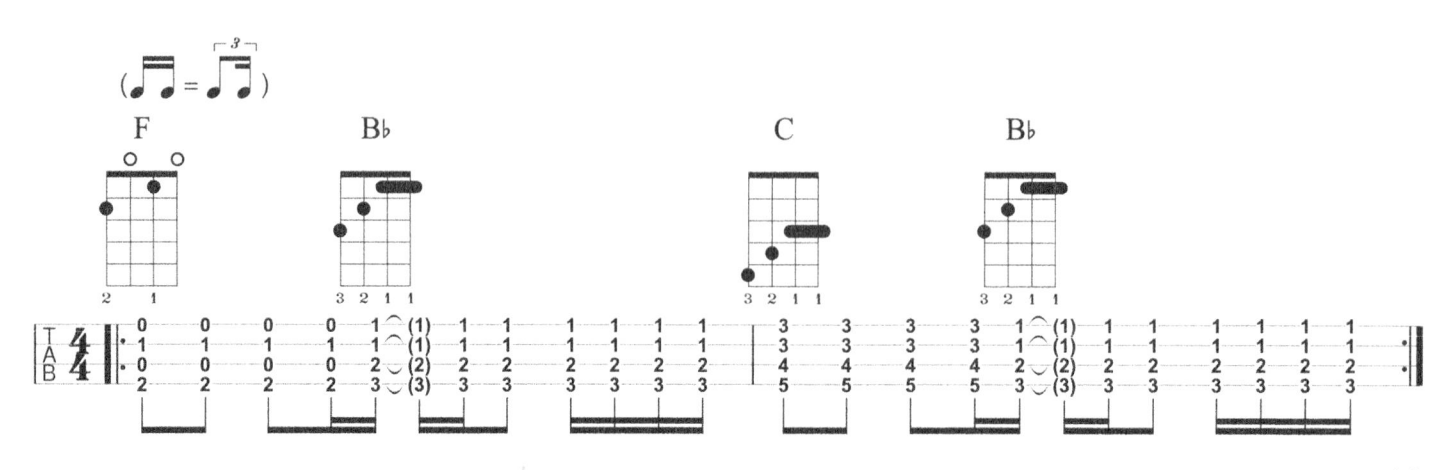

CHORD PROGRESSION: I–IV–vi–V (0:20–0:10)

Now let's take a look at the I–IV–vi–V progression. This is the progression that drives Grace VanderWaal's momentous ukulele hit "I Don't Know My Name," as well as songs like Twenty-One Pilots' "House of Gold," Boston's "More Than a Feeling," the Killers' "Mr. Brightside," and Sheryl Crow's "Strong Enough."

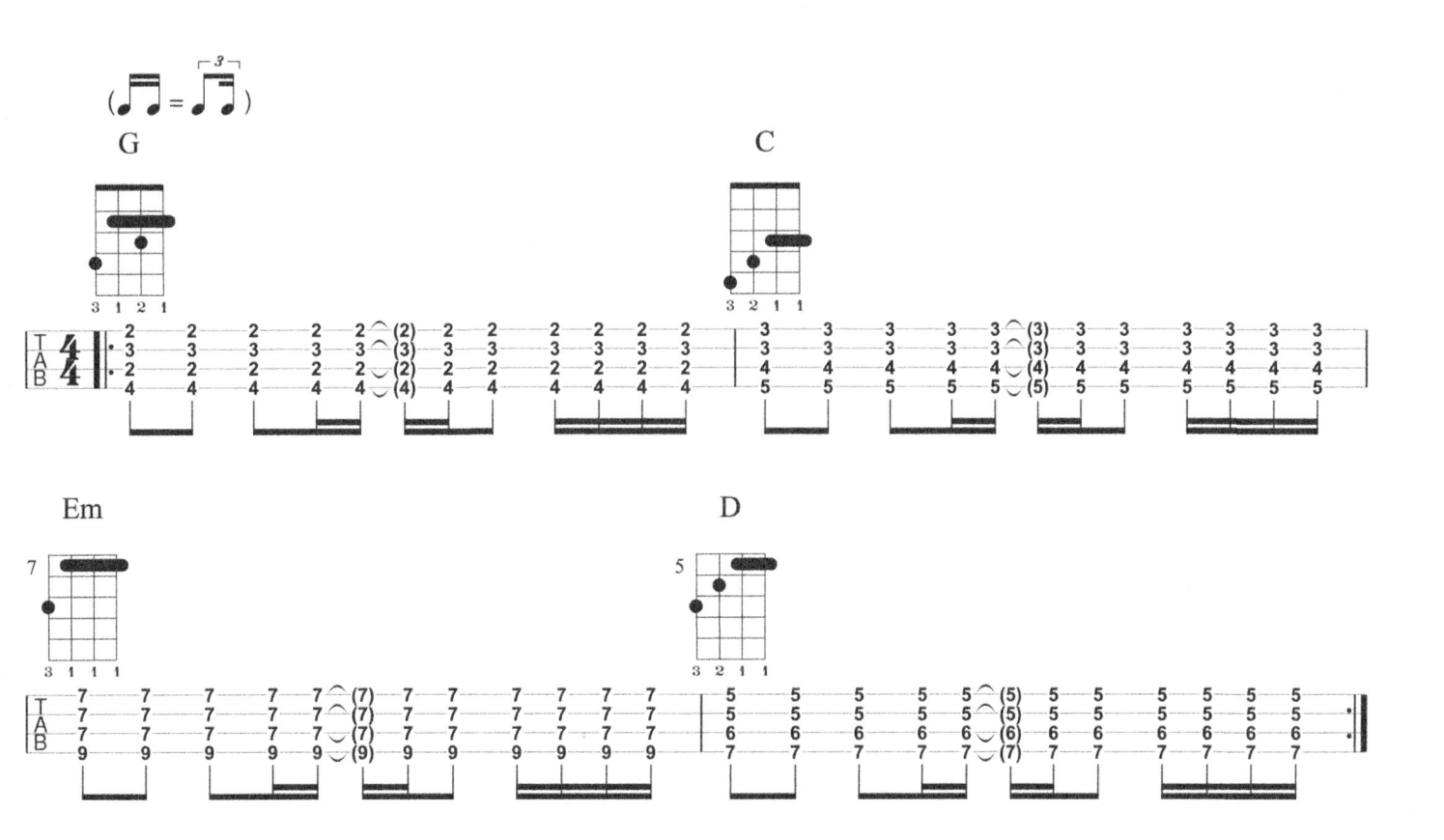

45

TECHNIQUE: FINGERSTYLE CHORD PLUCKING (0:10–0:00) 🔊

Earlier in this book, you learned how use the fingerstyle technique to play single notes, both for melodic lines and scales, as well as in the context of arpeggios. But you can also use your fingers to *pluck* chords, whereby you play four notes at once, or perhaps just three or two, or even the piano-style approach of alternating a single note from a chord with two other notes from the chord. The example below features a I–vi–ii–V progression that is very popular in jazz songs like "I Got Rhythm" and "Heart and Soul."

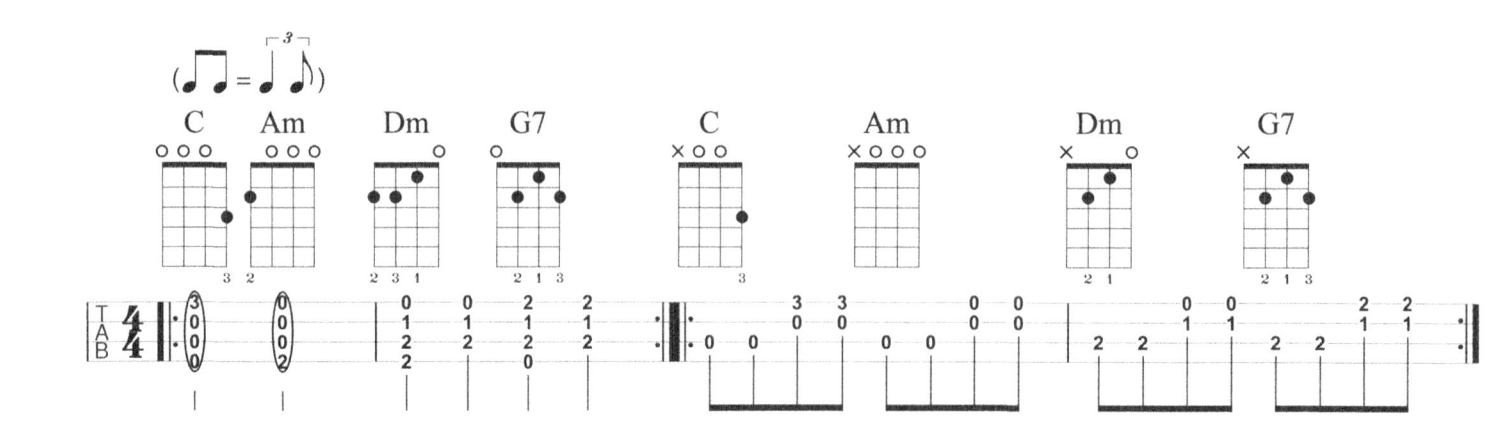

46

DAY 12

MAJOR CHORD (1:00–0:50) 🔊

Here's a movable major triad shape based on the open D chord—but only on the top three strings. The root for this shape is on the 3rd string. Use your index finger on the 1st string, ring finger on 3rd string, and pinky finger on the 2nd string. For added interest, you can include the open 4th string on every strum. This is called a *drone*, which is a note that is allowed to ring against all the other notes or chords in a passage.

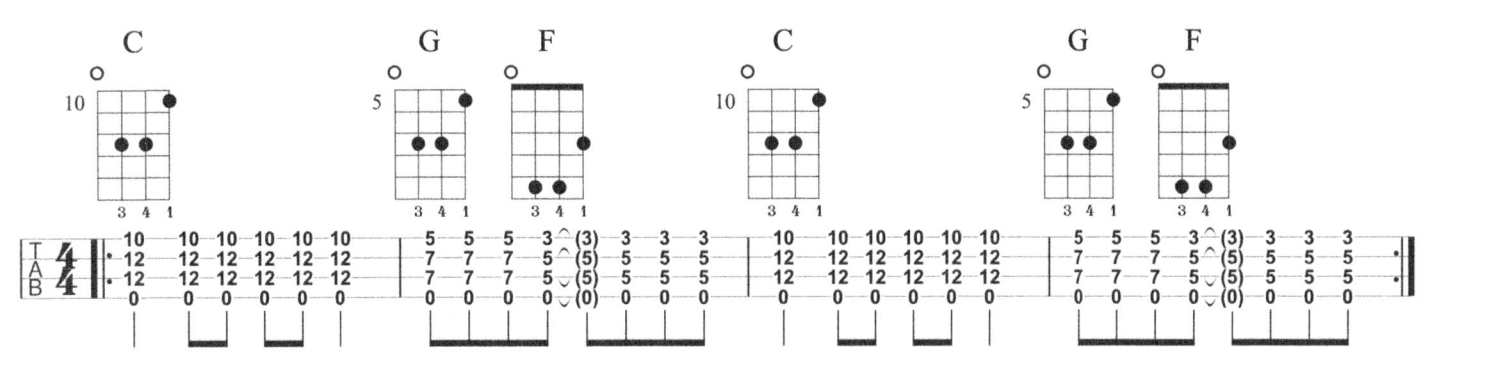

MINOR CHORD (0:50–0:40) 🔊

Remember the open E minor chord you learned on Day 3? If you play that chord but omit the 4th string, it becomes the movable minor version of the major triad you just learned in the previous section. Like the major chord, however, feel free to experiment with including the open 4th string as a drone, using your ears to determine which positions work best with it.

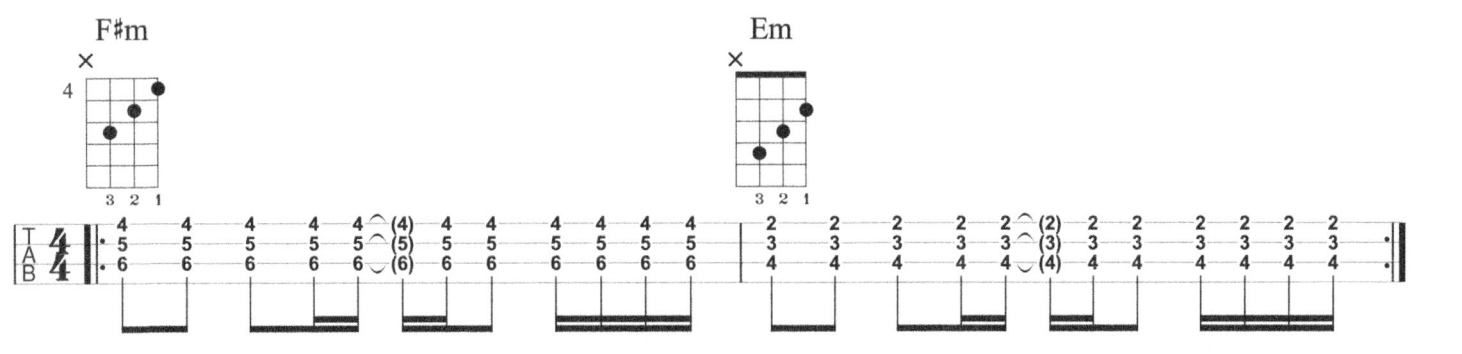

STRUM PATTERN (0:40–0:30) 🔊

This strum pattern is about as heavy on 16th notes as you'll find. It's a pattern of an eighth-plus-two-16ths followed by four 16th notes, repeating every two beats. It's the main strum pattern from Train's ukulele-based mega-hit "Hey, Soul Sister." Take care not to rush your strums—an easy pitfall when strumming so many 16th notes continuously.

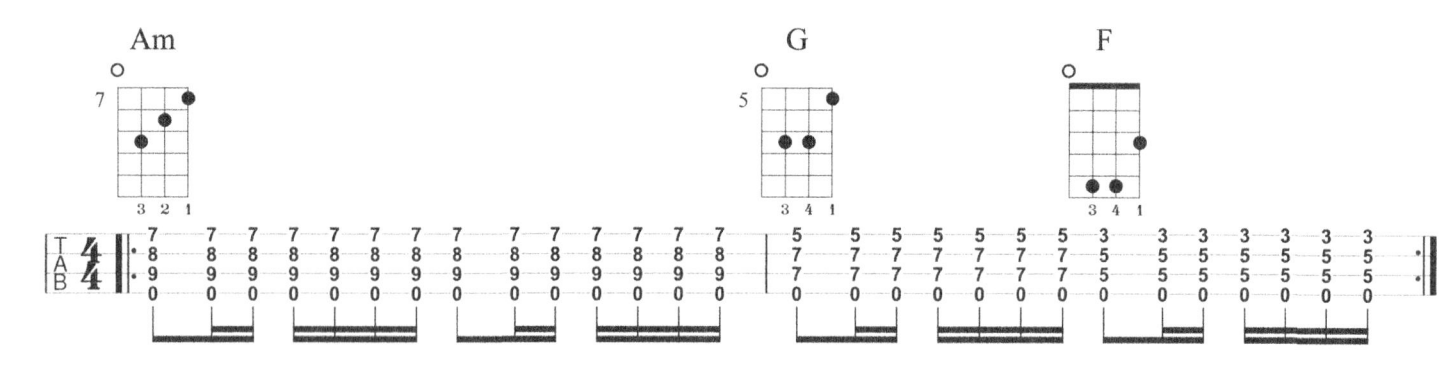

CHORD PROGRESSION: I–V–vi–IV (0:30–0:20) 🔊

Now let's take a look at the I–V–vi–IV progression. In the key of E, the chords are E–B–C♯m–A. You'll hear the I–V–vi–IV progression in the aforementioned "Hey, Soul Sister," as well as in Journey's "Don't Stop Believin'," Jason Mraz's "I'm Yours," Darius Rucker's "Wagon Wheel," and the chorus of "Let It Go" from Disney's *Frozen*.

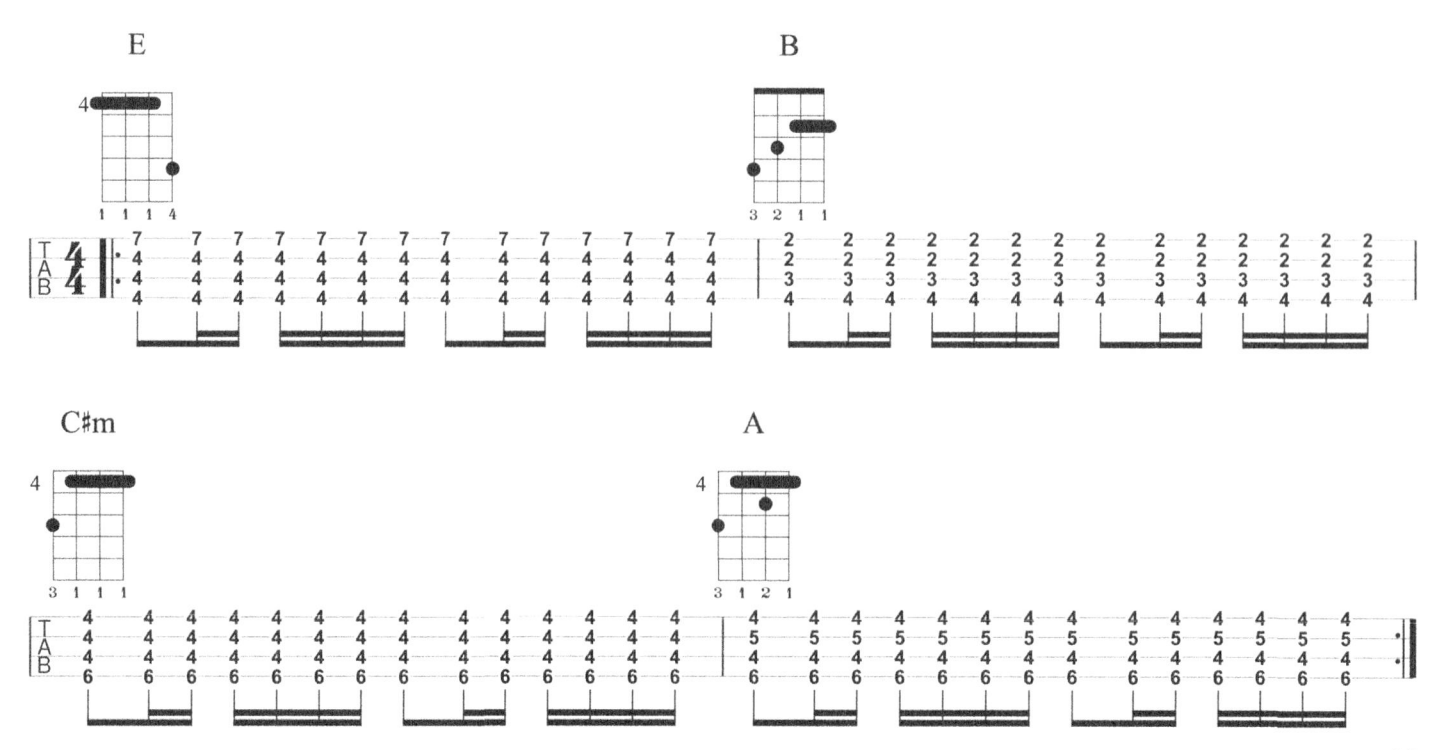

CHORD PROGRESSION: vi–IV–I–V (0:20–0:10)

Next up is the vi–IV–I–V, which you'll hear in Ed Sheeran's "Photograph," Eagle-Eye Cherry's "Save Tonight," and Green Day's "Boulevard of Broken Dreams." Note that this progression is the same as the I–V–vi–IV in the previous section, except it starts on the vi chord. In doing so, the progression evokes a minor-key sound.

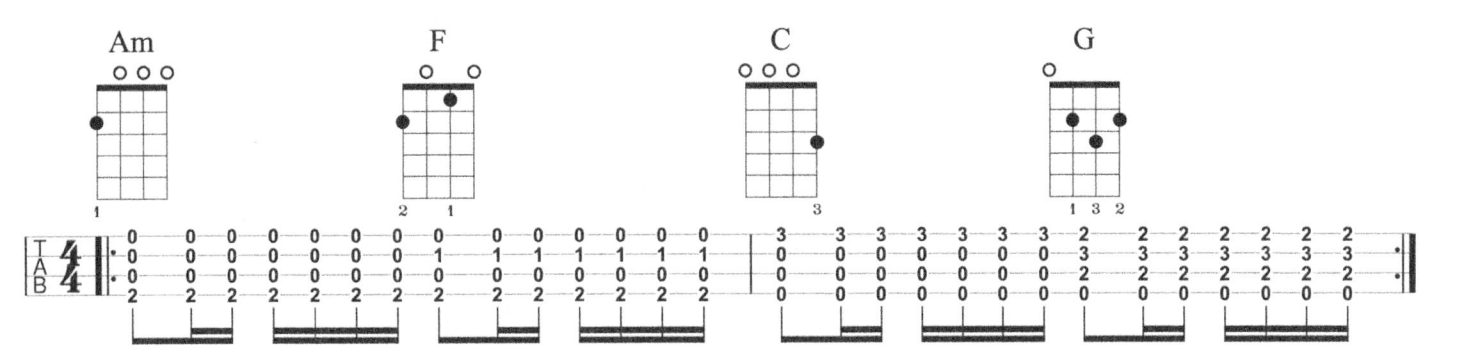

TECHNIQUE: ROLL STROKE (0:10–0:00)

The *roll stroke* is a special strum typically used to emphasize the downbeat and is performed by "unrolling" in rapid succession each of your pick-hand fingers, from a loose fist position to an open hand. The result of the action is four attacks that sound like one continuous strum. Listen to the accompanying audio to hear how this technique should sound.

If you're not able to play the roll stroke in the example below right away—and you probably won't—try this exercise: While muting all four strings with your fret hand, form a loose fist with your strumming hand, and then "flick" just your pinky across all four strings for a muted strum. Do this about 4–8 times, then add your ring finger so that your flicking your pinky, *immediately* followed by your ring finger. After 4–8 repetitions, add your middle finger and, finally, your index finger.

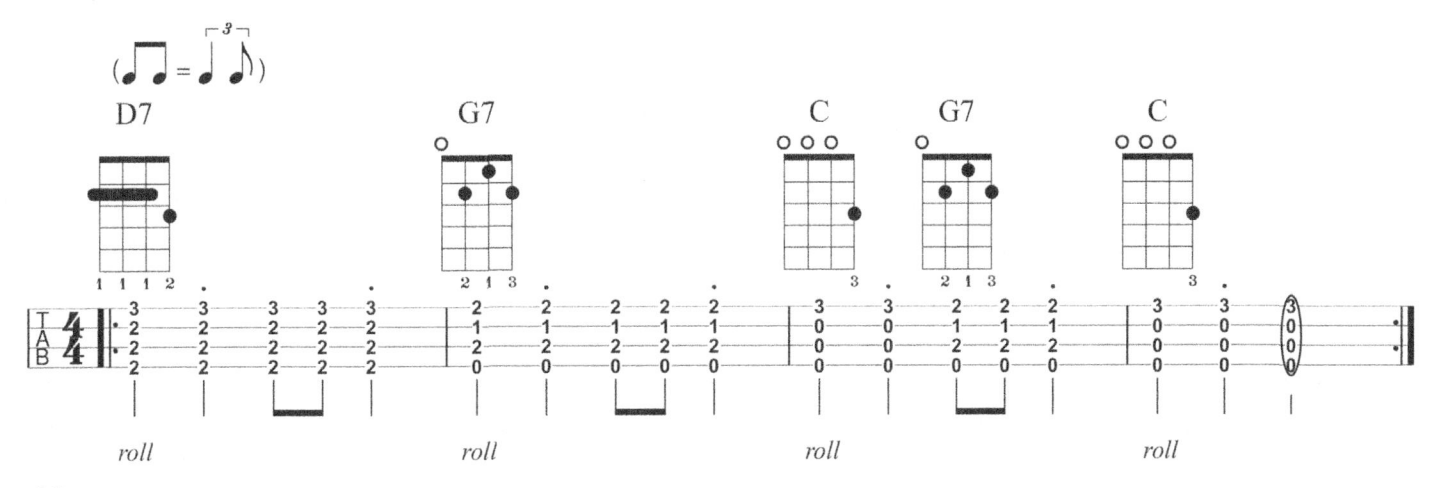

49

DAY 13

MAJOR CHORD (1:00–0:50) 🔊

This last "major" chord is actually in a category all by itself. The *augmented* chord is the same as a major chord, except the 5th degree of the chord is raised a half step, or one fret. Interestingly, any one of the three notes in an augmented chord can serve as the root note, so the chord repeats itself every four frets; that is, using the shape shown below, you can play a C augmented chord (Caug) at the 3rd fret, 7th fret, or 11th fret. If you find it too difficult at first to get your pinky finger around to the 4th string, you can omit it entirely and just play the top three strings. You can hear the augmented chord in the intros to Chuck Berry's "School Days" and the Beatles' "Oh, Darling."

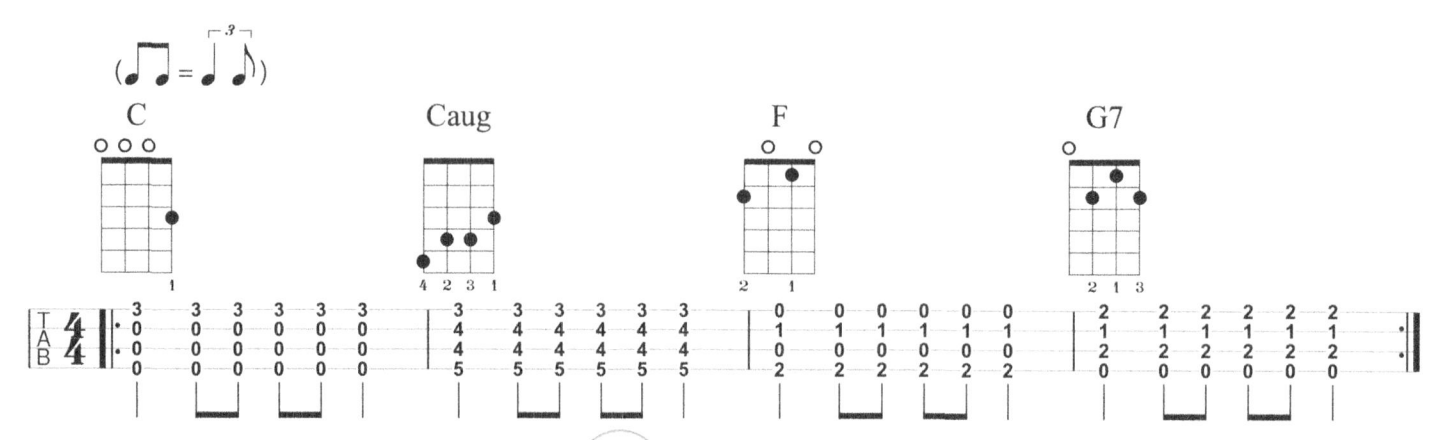

MINOR CHORD (0:50–0:40) 🔊

Like the augmented chord from the previous section, the diminished chord is really an entity unto itself. And similar to the augmented chord, any one of the diminished chord's four notes can serve as the root, which means the chord repeats itself every three frets. The diminished chord typically precedes the I chord, as in the example below, although, because of its dissonant nature, it's a very effective tool for building suspense, as you'll see in today's final example.

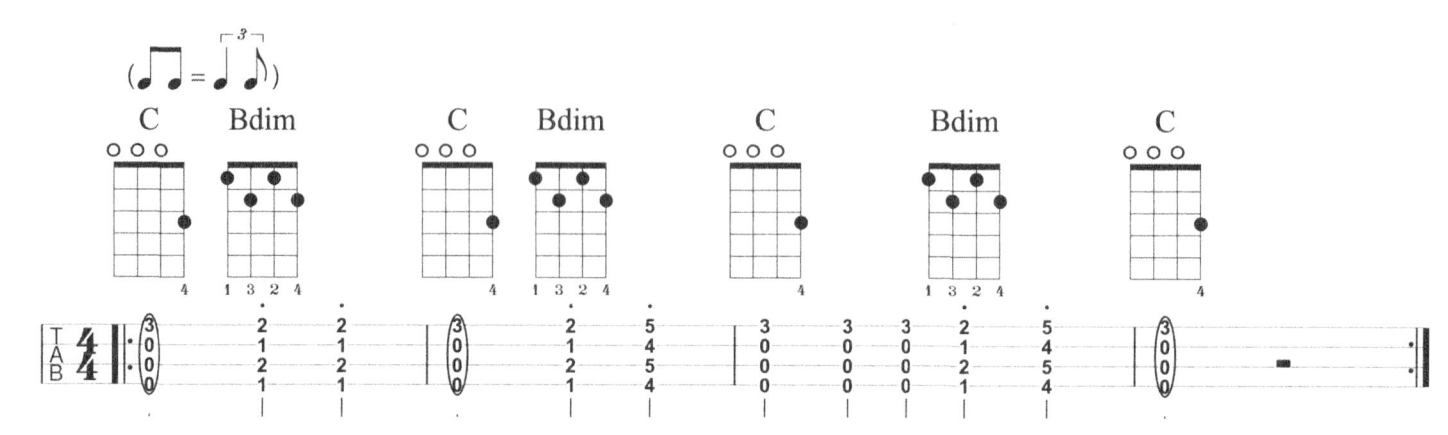

50

STRUM PATTERN (0:40–0:30) 🔊

Aside from 4/4, the 6/8 time signature is the one most commonly heard in popular music. Strictly speaking, 6/8 time contains six eighth notes per measure, but the pulse is felt as two beats per measure, or as a pair of dotted quarter notes. So, you might count it as: **1**–2–3, **4**–5–6, with beats 1 and 4 serving as downbeats. You can certainly strum a 6/8 song using that very pattern of one strum per eighth note, but the variation below, where beats 1 and 4 are eighth notes, and beats 2, 3, 5, and 6 each comprise pairs of 16th notes, is more common—especially in pop and rock ballads.

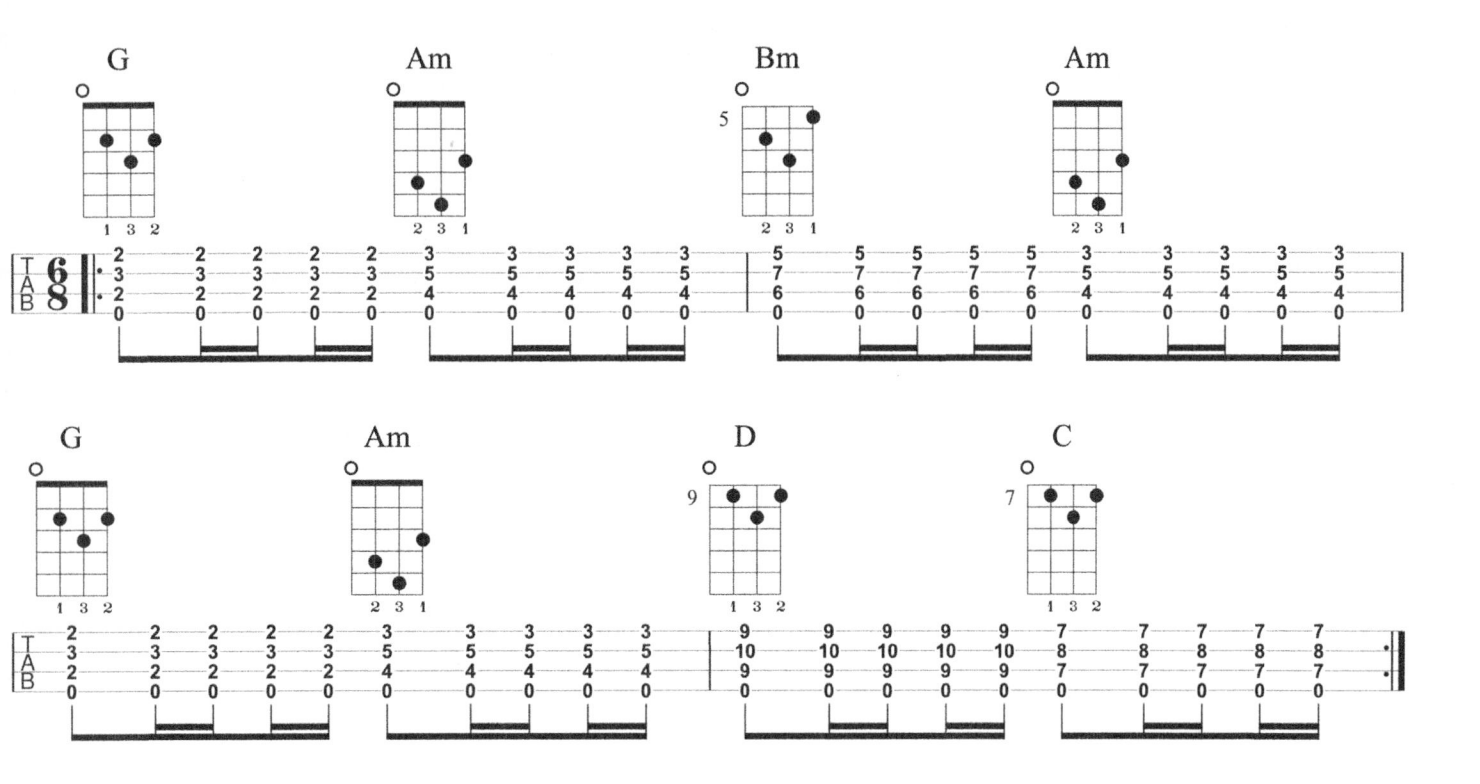

CHORD PROGRESSION: I–vi–IV–V (0:30–0:20) 🔊

The I–vi–IV–V chord progression is essential learning. You'll hear it in timeless oldies like "Unchained Melody" by the Righteous Brothers, "Earth Angel" by the Penguins, and "Stand by Me" by Ben E. King, classic rockers such as "Crocodile Rock" by Elton John and "Every Breath You Take" by the Police, and modern hits like "Baby" by Justin Bieber and "Me!" by Taylor Swift and Brendan Urie.

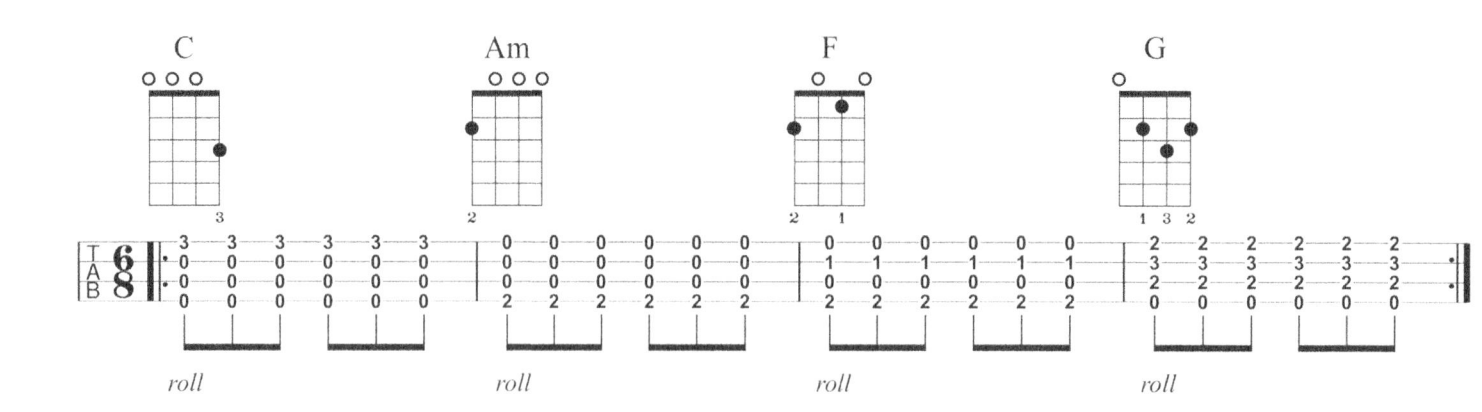

```
        C                    Am                   F                    G

T  6 |:-3--3--3--3--3--3---0--0--0--0--0--0---0--0--0--0--0--0---2--2--2--2--2--2--:|
A  8 |:-0--0--0--0--0--0---0--0--0--0--0--0---1--1--1--1--1--1---3--3--3--3--3--3--:|
B    |:-0--0--0--0--0--0---0--0--0--0--0--0---0--0--0--0--0--0---2--2--2--2--2--2--:|
     |:-0--0--0--0--0--0---2--2--2--2--2--2---2--2--2--2--2--2---0--0--0--0--0--0--:|
         roll                 roll                 roll                 roll
```

52

CHORD PROGRESSION: I–V–ii–IV (0:20–0:10)

Your final chord progression is the I–V–ii–IV, which you can hear in Taylor Swift's "You Belong With Me," The Cure's "Just Like Heaven," Smash Mouth's "All Star," and Katy Perry's "Hot N Cold."

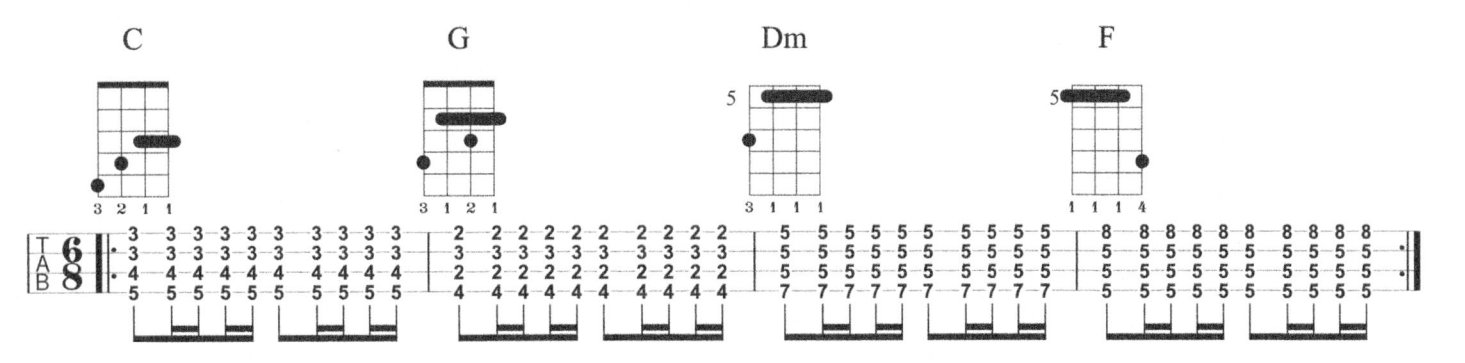

TECHNIQUE: TREMOLO STRUM (0:10–0:00)

Another useful ukulele technique is the *tremolo* strum, whereby you strum in up and down fashion as fast as you can while holding down a chord or note. You'll typically use this strum on the penultimate chord of a song when you're performing live—sort of the "big finish."

To perform a tremolo strum, hold your index finger perpendicular to the strings and rotate your wrist up and down in a rapid yet relaxed fashion, brushing the strings just hard enough to sound the chord. Try to keep your forearm relaxed, as it's very easy to tense up while using this technique, and that will lead not only to poor execution but also potential pain and injury. In the example below, you'll apply the tremolo to the four inversions of the diminished chord you learned earlier today.

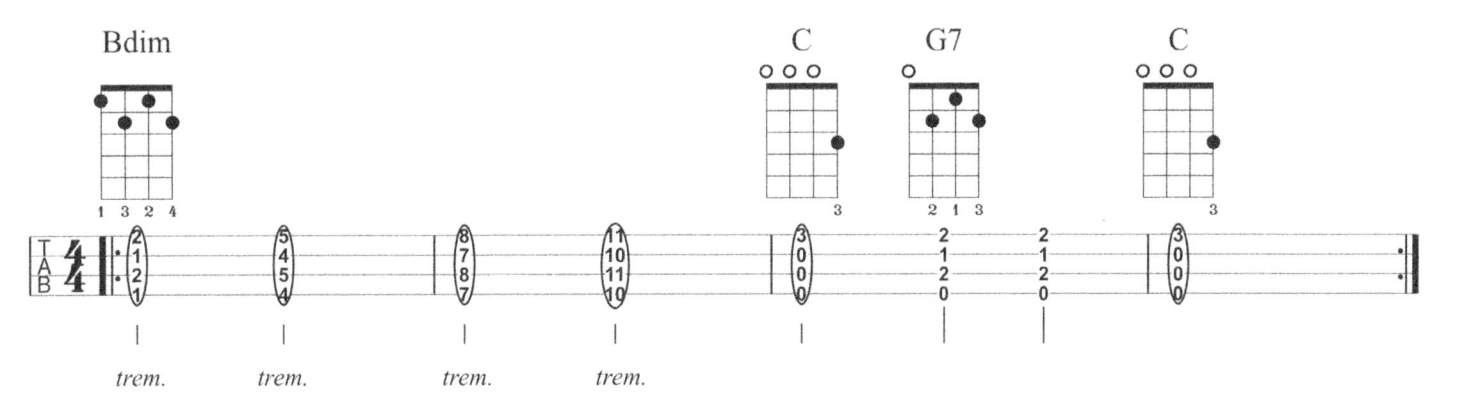

DAY 14 – WEEK 2 REVIEW: PUTTING IT ALL TOGETHER

"AMAZING GRACE" CHORD MELODY (1:00–0:00) 🔊

Congratulations—you've made it to Day 14! And, if you've been faithfully practicing the examples, you have all the essential tools needed to play your favorite songs on the ukulele. Today's task is an introduction to *chord melody,* whereby you'll combine chords and single notes to play an easy arrangement of "Amazing Grace." On the audio example, you'll hear techniques such as regular strums and single-note picking, as well as chord plucks, roll strums, and tremolo. While playing the song, feel free to apply in your own imaginative ways the various techniques you've learned. Remember: music is about expressing yourself, so don't be afraid to experiment.

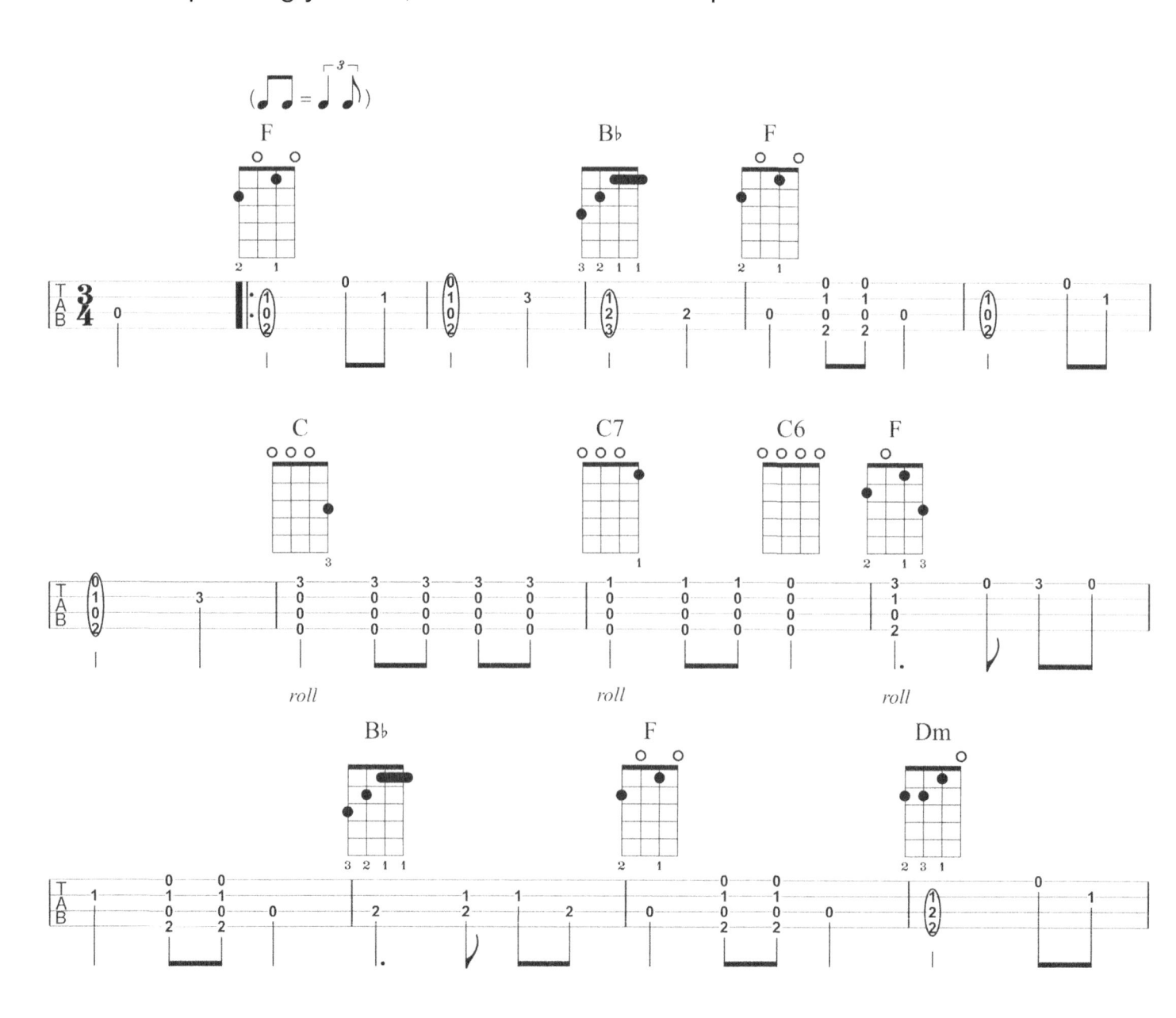

54

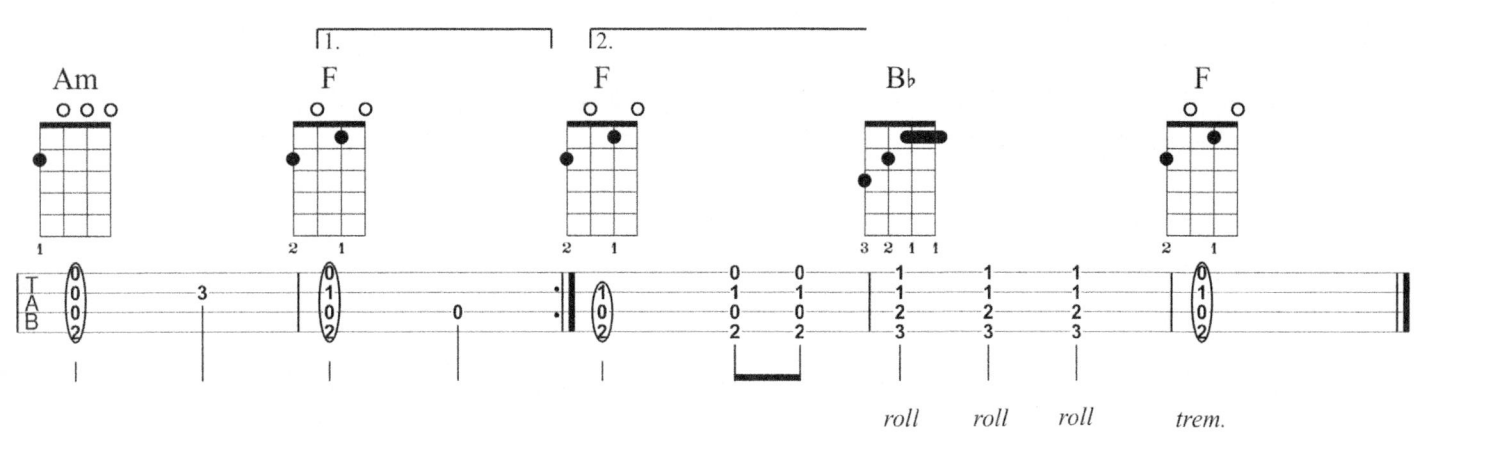

MOVING FORWARD

If you've reached this page, you've learned much of what you need to know to play your favorite songs. Remember to keep practicing the techniques you learned here so that you will eventually play with great confidence, which results in a superior performance.

Below is one final chart to help you either in learning existing songs or in writing your own. It contains *chord families* for popular ukulele keys. To learn how to play actual songs, you can find chords and lyric charts for just about any song you could possibly want to play via Internet sites or printed music books. It's all pretty much right at your fingertips.

CHORD FAMILIES FOR POPULAR UKULELE KEYS

CHORD:	I	ii	iii	IV	V (V7)	vi	vii°
KEY OF C	C	Dm	Em	F	G (G7)	Am	B°
KEY OF F	F	Gm	Am	Bb	C (C7)	Dm	E°
KEY OF G	G	Am	Bm	C	D (D7)	Em	F#°
KEY OF A	A	Bm	C#m	D	E (E7)	F#m	G#°
KEY OF D	D	Em	F#m	G	A (A7)	Bm	C#°
KEY OF E	E	F#m	G#m	A	B (B7)	C#m	D#°

Printed in Great Britain
by Amazon